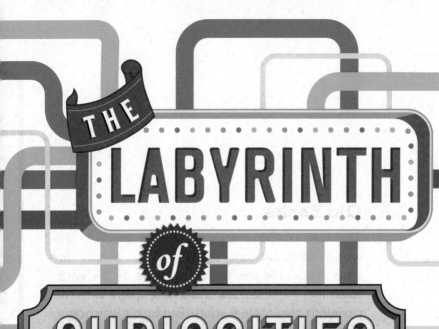

# THE LABYRINTH of CURIOSITIES

**JOURNEY THROUGH HUNDREDS OF WILD FACTS AND FASCINATING TRIVIA— AND THEIR SURPRISING CONNECTIONS!**

## Fay Moss-Rider

Odd Dot ⦿⦿ New York

## Old Books

*The Epic of Gilgamesh*, the oldest book in the world, tells the story of a king on a hunt for immortality. He travels to the ends of the earth to collect a miraculous underwater plant with the power to give eternal youth. But on his way home, a snake steals it and gives all snakes the power to shed old skin for new.

**Miraculous Plants**
**Crazy Anti-Aging Techniques**
**Thieving Snakes**

## Miraculous Plants

After the great Tokyo earthquake of 1923, people noticed the only trees that survived the resulting fires were ginkgos. So the Japanese began to plant ginkgo trees all over the country, which is how ginkgo trees were planted in Hiroshima, where they not only lived through the A-bomb dropped in 1945 but bloomed the very next year.

**Earthshaking**

## Crazy Anti-Aging Techniques

Greeks and Romans used to make facial masks out of crocodile dung and even paid extra to get submerged in baths full of it, certain that it would help them stay young.

**Strange Baths**

## Thieving Snakes

Most snakes avoid eating toads because they might be poisonous. But Japanese grass snakes don't just eat poisonous toads—they absorb the toads' poison to use in their own snake venom.

**Unlucky Toads**

## Earthshaking

The worst earthquake in recorded history hit the Chilean city of Valdivia in 1960, with a magnitude of 9.5. It disrupted the seafloor so much that boats were damaged in Los Angeles and San Diego, and fifteen hours later, when waves from the Chilean coast reached Hawaii, 6,200 miles away, they were still 35 feet high.

**Big Waves**

## Strange Baths

In medieval times, the rules at Westminster Abbey only required monks to bathe four times a year, including Easter and Christmas. But the monks might not have been as dirty as that might make them sound: historical records show that a bath attendant was on duty all year round.

**Christmas Traditions**

## Unlucky Toads

Surinam toads don't lay their eggs, then wander off and leave them, as some other toads do. These toad moms carry fertilized eggs under the skin of their back. When the eggs start to hatch, the arms of tiny toads begin to punch free through mom's skin, with as many as a hundred hatching at a time.

**Too Many Eggs**

# Christmas Traditions

Anyone who wanted to stay on the right side of the law in seventeenth-century England and Scotland had to avoid practicing Christmas traditions for almost two decades, from 1644 to 1660. Why? Some Christmas festivities were seen as pagan customs by the church and could lead to charges of witchcraft. So Christmas carols were illegal in the British Isles, and today's popular classics "The First Noel" and "God Rest Ye Merry, Gentlemen" almost disappeared from history, until eighteenth-century and Victorian carol collectors revived the tradition.

**Warding Off Witchcraft**

# Big Waves

Captain James Cook wrote about watching a Hawaiian man ride waves around the islands in 1778, the first time surfing was ever recorded in writing. But he might not have realized that what he was watching wasn't a game to Hawaiians. It was part of their religious tradition.

**Far-Flung States**

# Warding Off Witchcraft

Holy water, salt, and mistletoe have all been used to ward off witches, but by Victorian times, more sophisticated methods had been developed: many people hung brightly colored glass "witch balls" in their windows to catch evil spells before they could sneak in.

**Incredible Salt**

# Too Many Eggs

A two-person New Zealand team broke the world record for the longest egg toss in 2017, with a successful throw of more than 80 meters—or just over 262 feet! Their record-breaking toss took place at the annual World Egg Throwing Championships in Swaton, England, a village that claims to be the site of the first egg toss in history, when local monks threw eggs over a flooded river to feed hungry townsfolk, in 1322.

**Helpful Monks**

# Far-Flung States

The southernmost state in the United States is Hawaii. The northernmost, westernmost, and easternmost state is Alaska. It's easy to understand how Alaska is the northernmost and westernmost. But how is it the easternmost? Because Alaska's Aleutian Islands cross the 180th meridian, meaning that some of them are in the Eastern Hemisphere.

**New States**

## Helpful Monks

Some Tibetan monks have so much mental control of their physical being that they can raise their body temperature—enough to dry wet sheets that are wrapped around them.

**Crazy Temperature Changes**

## New States

Alaska and Hawaii were the last two states to join the Union— Alaska in January 1959, and Hawaii in August 1959.

**Summer of '59**

## Incredible Salt

A huge salt mine lies directly under the city of Detroit, more than 1,000 feet belowground. It's been in continuous operation for over a century, and its 1,500 subterranean acres are served by over 100 miles of hidden roads.

**Underground Roads**

## Crazy Temperature Changes

On a single day in 1911—November 11—Kansas City and Oklahoma City recorded both record high and record low temperatures for the date, as the most extreme cold front ever recorded in the United States swept across the plains. In Kansas City, the mercury dropped from 76 to 11 degrees Fahrenheit. And in Oklahoma City, temperatures plunged from 83 to 17.

**Record Highs**

## Summer of '59

On the last day of August 1959, in the heart of a heat wave, five hundred blocks of Manhattan went dark for thirteen hours. Jukeboxes went silent, and café patrons ate by candlelight. The likely culprit: overly enthusiastic use of an invention that had only recently become widely available, the air conditioner.

**Name That Box**

## Record Highs

In 2017, soprano Audrey Luna sang the highest note ever hit by anyone in the history of New York City's Metropolitan Opera: an A above high C, as part of a passage where the music mimics laughter. When the recording was broadcast over the radio, dogs around the world reportedly barked in response.

**Underground Opera**

## Underground Roads

Lots of American cities sit atop abandoned train tunnels, drain passages, or even service tunnels used to smuggle liquor during Prohibition. But Chicago probably has the country's most complicated underground maze, with six different tunnel systems built for pedestrians, commuter trains, cable cars, tiny freight trains, drinking water, and rain runoff.

**Underground Opera**

## Name That Box

Jukeboxes got their name from juke joints, small local bars that featured music and dancing. And *juke* comes from a Gullah word that means "rowdy"—or "wicked."

**Rowdy Theaters**

## Underground Opera

The Paris Opera house was built on a marsh, too damp to drain. So the architect Charles Garnier constructed a giant cistern under the theater to catch the encroaching groundwater and serve as a reservoir in case of fire. Today, Paris firefighters still do their underwater training in the eerie underground lake.

**Rowdy Theaters**

## Rowdy Theaters

In May 1849, fans of the American actor Edwin Forrest bought hundreds of tickets to the balcony of Manhattan's Astor Opera House and interrupted the performance of his English rival, William Charles Macready, by throwing lemons, eggs, potatoes, apples, shoes, and even theater seats at the stage. It wasn't just that they didn't like Macready's interpretation of *Macbeth*—the two actors had become symbols for growing tensions between Americans and the English. When Macready took the stage again three days later, ten thousand people crowded around the theater, while others inside tried unsuccessfully to set it on fire. Government troops opened fire on the crowd, killing between twenty-two and thirty-one of them, and wounding almost fifty others, a tragedy that forced the theater to close the following year.

**Firefighting Actors**
**Flying Lemons**
**Flying Potatoes**

## Firefighting Actors

Steve Buscemi is a beloved character actor, with star turns in *Boardwalk Empire* and *Fargo*, but his first job was as a firefighter: he served four years with New York's Engine Company 55 in Little Italy, starting in 1980.

**Little Italy**

## Flying Lemons

Dorothy "Dot" Lemon was a barnstorming aviator in the 1920s, ran a flight school in Florida with her husband, and became the first woman president of the Institute of Navigation in 1961. But those may or may not have been her most interesting accomplishments: she also claimed to be the first person to deliberately fly into the eye of a hurricane.

**Tornado Potatoes**

## Flying Potatoes

During the Irish potato famine, from 1845 to 1849, desperate people sometimes jumped from the cliffs as boats headed out of harbor for England, hoping to land on deck—but almost none of them made it. English sailors nicknamed the jumps potato flying—and today the phrase *potato flying* still refers to trying something but failing.

**Tornado Potatoes**

## Tornado Potatoes

South Korea boasts a popular street food called tornado fries: spiralized potatoes deep-fried on long skewers. They come seasoned with everything from honey to cheese, and some are even embellished with slices of sausage.

**Roman Street Food**

## Little Italy

The theme park Italy in Miniature, in Rimini, contains almost three hundred miniatures of the grand architectural treasures of Italy. Visitors don't have to travel the whole Italian peninsula to see all the sights: here, the pint-sized version of Rome's Colosseum is within walking distance of the micro-replica of Venice's Grand Canal, and just down the way from the tiny but intricate Duomo of Milan. All this, *and* a catapult ride that will shoot you almost 200 feet in less than two seconds— plus Europe's very first monorail.

**Unusual Uses for Catapults**
**Roman Street Food**

# Roman Street Food

Street food isn't a modern invention: ancient Romans ate salted peas while cheering on the gladiators at the Colosseum, and bought sausages, figs, and stews served in jars on the street, with spiced wine to wash it all down.

## Putting Stuff in Jars

# Unusual Uses for Catapults

You might think that catapults went out of fashion along with medieval wimples for covering a lady's hair, but the U.S. Navy still uses them to launch aircraft from the decks of carriers. And the city of Aspen in Colorado is taking no chances: it has a law on the books that makes it a crime to use a catapult to throw anything at any property within the city limits.

## Extreme Hairdos

## Extreme Hairdos

Early punk rockers wanted their hair to stand straight up, and sometimes no commercial spray was up to the job, so they used everything from egg whites to glue to get the perfect Mohawk or spikes.

**Weird Ingredients**

## Putting Stuff in Jars

Albert Einstein didn't want his brain studied, but when he died, the doctor on call at Princeton Hospital stole it and kept it in a pair of jars that he stored in a cider box under a beer cooler, until the doctor's heirs finally donated it to the National Museum of Health and Medicine.

**Dishonest Doctors**

## Dishonest Doctors
## Weird Ingredients

The United States didn't get into the business of drug regulation until 1906, long after laws had been passed to promote the purity of oleomargarine (1886), meat (1891), and tea (1897). Until then, quack doctors drove from town to town peddling "patent medicine" in bright bottles that promised to cure rabies with opium, sore throats with cocaine, and liver disease with turpentine. Some of their wares survive on our shelves today, including petroleum jelly, which used to be touted as a treatment for burns, blindness, and skin ulcers; Coca-Cola, which was famously laced with cocaine; and Dr Pepper, originally touted as a "brain tonic."

**Successful Quacks**
**Brain Tonic**
**Antique Margarine**

## Successful Quacks

The World's Championship Duck Calling Contest has been held on Thanksgiving weekend in Stuttgart, Arkansas, every year since 1936. Local duck callers created it to settle an argument over which one of them made the best duck calls. Today it draws callers from around the world, who compete for the title with a single ninety-second routine.

**Bird Brains**

## Brain Tonic

Want to activate your brain to produce nutrients that help memory and resist aging? Your brain likes new experiences that have both emotional and physical elements, like brushing your teeth with the wrong hand, turning your clock upside down, sitting at a new seat at a familiar table, or reading aloud to a friend.

**Bird Brains**

## Antique Margarine

When margarine was invented in 1869, it was cheaper than butter—and lasted longer. But the dairy industry fought back. Margarine was banned in New York, Maine, Michigan, and much of the Midwest. In other states only *yellow* margarine was illegal, which meant people had to use golden dye packets at home to turn the white goop buttery. And laws in Vermont, South Dakota, and New Hampshire required margarine to be dyed pink!

### Pink Food

## Bird Brains

Crows are generally considered among the world's smartest birds. They can make tools, count objects, think about other creatures' emotions, and recognize human faces. They've even been known to use bread crumbs to lure fish—or swipe fishermen's lines to pull hooked fish out of the water. And they're not just smarter than other birds: on intelligence tests, they even beat apes.

### Dumb Apes

## Pink Food

The watermelon is one of the world's oldest cultivated fruits, with tomb drawings indicating that Egyptians grew them over five thousand years ago. Their water content is so high—92 percent—that some travelers used to carry watermelon instead of water. The Chinese grow the most watermelons in the world today, although the plant originated in Africa. But the Japanese may have the most interesting cultivation technique: they grow square watermelons by planting them in wooden boxes.

**Surprising Tombs**
**Agricultural Hacks**

## Dumb Apes

Why don't apes talk, anyway? They have vocal cords that could make the same sounds as those used in human speech. But even though some primates have famously learned sign language, it turns out that the great apes don't have the mental power to string spoken sentences together.

**Sign Language Puns**

## Surprising Tombs

A recently discovered Egyptian tomb didn't just house mummified royals. The tomb, just outside Cairo, contained mummies of cats, scarab beetles, cobras, and crocodiles, all precisely preserved, and undisturbed for the past 4,500 years.

**Zombie Cats**

## Agricultural Hacks

Chinese farmers are famous for growing rice in beautiful tiered pools. Less well-known is the super-efficient practice of farming fish in the same water. Rice plants shade the fish and protect them from predators, while fish fertilize the plants, reduce weeds, and eat harmful larvae. The result: more rice and more fish than if either were farmed separately.

**Novel Fishing Techniques**

## Sign Language Puns

American Sign Language is full of puns. Want to sign *Shakespeare*? Make the sign for *spear*—then shake it. And if you want to sign *microwave*, just lift your pinkie and wiggle it. Get it? It's a *micro* wave!

**Shakespearean Cats**

## Zombie Cats

Cats may or may not have nine lives, but some of them seem to be among the walking dead. In 2019, a cat named Fluffy was rescued from a snowbank in Montana with a temperature so low it didn't budge the vet's thermometer. But hours later, with the help of heating pads and a warm bath, she was moving around—and back to her regular self within a week.

**Shakespearean Cats**

## Novel Fishing Techniques

In 1607, when Captain John Smith arrived in Chesapeake Bay, he recorded sailing through a school of fish called menhaden, "lying so thick with their heads above the water, as for want of nets (our barge driving amongst them) we attempted to catch them with a frying pan."

**Surprises at Sea**

## Shakespearean Cats

Hate cats? So did Shakespeare. They're mentioned in many of his plays, including *Romeo and Juliet*, where Mercutio insults Tybalt by calling him the "king of cats," and *A Midsummer Night's Dream*, in which Lysander spits, "Hang off, thou cat, thou burr! Vile thing." Cats make appearances in *Henry IV*, *The Merry Wives of Windsor*, and even *Coriolanus*, but Shakespeare never has one nice thing to say about them. The closest he comes to a cat compliment is in *The Merchant of Venice*, when Shylock allows there might be such a thing as "a harmless necessary cat."

**Merry Wives**

## Surprises at Sea

Scientists thought sailors were telling tall tales when they swapped stories about rogue waves: monsters that seemed to come out of nowhere on a relatively calm sea. But in 1995, they finally found out the hard way, when an oil platform off the coast of Norway was hit by a gargantuan 84-foot wave on an otherwise-normal ocean.

**Wave Length**
**Mythical Rogues**

## Merry Wives

What's the best way for a man to have a happy life? Have a happy wife. Turns out, the old adage is true. In a giant study that combed through information from eighteen thousand people, the best predictor of how happy a man was with his life was how happy *his wife* was with their marriage—whether he felt he was living in a state of wedded bliss, or not.

### Surprising Husbands

## Mythical Rogues

Han Solo, James Bond, and Rhett Butler are all rogues we love to hate or hate to love, but the Western world's original mythical rogue may be Sir Lancelot. He's best known for stealing the affections of King Arthur's wife, Guinevere. Less well-known is the fact that he also fathered Sir Galahad. Galahad became known as the purest of all knights, despite—or perhaps because of—his father's bad reputation.

### Famous Bachelors

## Famous Bachelors
## Surprising Husbands

James Bond's known as the consummate bachelor, but in the 1963 novel *On Her Majesty's Secret Service*, by Bond creator Ian Fleming, he does marry Tracy Draco, a countess who wins his heart after her father offers Bond his considerable resources to track down one of Bond's archenemies, Ernst Stavro Blofeld. But on their wedding day, Blofeld tracks down Bond and kills Tracy—and Bond, in his grief, hardens into the famous international man of mystery.

**Lady Spies**

## Wave Length

Ever feel like no one thinks like you? Turns out, you're right. Scientists say that our brain waves may be as unique as our fingerprints. But that doesn't mean no one will ever "get" you: brain-wave studies show that when friends watch the same film clips, they have remarkably similar patterns of brain waves, compared to strangers.

**Unique Fingerprints**

## Unique Fingerprints

Humans aren't the only creatures with unique fingerprints: chimps and gorillas have one-of-a-kind fingertips as well, which kind of makes sense, since they're also primates. A little more surprising is the only other known animal with individual fingerprints: the cuddly koala bear.

**Remarkable Bears**

## Remarkable Bears

Bears have incredible memories, especially when it comes to sweets. When trains filled with sweet syrup or corn meal crash, bears have been known to assist vigorously with the cleanup, which they see as a feast. Not only that, but they'll return hopefully to the scene of the sweets for as long as they live.

**Spying on Bears**
**Crazy Train Crashes**
**Sweet Teeth**

## Lady Spies

Mary Bowser would have given James Bond a run for his money. Born into slavery, she was set free by Elizabeth "Bet" Van Lew, who built a Union spy ring in Richmond, Virginia, the Confederacy's capital city. Mary took a job as a maid in Jefferson Davis's house, pretending to be illiterate and slow, when in fact she could read and had a photographic memory. She read everything she could that came across Davis's desk, passing the secrets on to Union leadership—and perhaps contributing to Davis's mental breakdown over the course of the war. She fled to safety just before the end of the war, worried that someone in the Davis household might be onto her. And within months after the war ended, she was already teaching children who had been living in slavery how to read.

**Spying on Bears**
**More Than a Maid**

Mata Hari might be famous today simply for inventing the striptease—which she introduced to Europe as an exotic dancer during the early 1900s—if she hadn't also been executed as a spy. The charge: spying for the Germans during World War I, when she was a citizen of Paris. The details are still contested today, with some saying her trial was trumped up by the French to explain their own military defeats. But according to her own testimony, Mata Hari did trade information to the Germans for her freedom at the start of the war, when she was stuck in Amsterdam. But she also claimed her loyalties were always to the Allies—which bolsters the assertions of historians who believe she was a double agent.

**Spying on Bears**
**More Than a Maid**

Virginia Hall was a war correspondent for the *New York Post* in France during World War II, and also worked for the French Resistance. And she did it all with a prosthetic leg. She used its hollow interior to hide documents, and was so effective in the Resistance that she wound up on the Gestapo's most-wanted list.

**Spying on Bears**
**More Than a Maid**

## Spying on Bears

Polar bears travel huge distances in some of the harshest climates in the world, so they're notoriously hard for scientists to track. But high-tech innovations, including wireless-enabled collars and even satellites, have yielded some new insights on where the heck they go, and how, including the fact that they can swim for more than a week at a time. They've also started to rove places they never used to go, where some of them have begun to pair off with grizzlies, producing polar-grizzly cubs.

**Difficult Tracking**

## Crazy Train Crashes

When a Walter L. Main Circus train flew off the tracks while taking a curve in the wilds of Pennsylvania in May 1893, hundreds of animals—including camels, elephants, zebras, tigers, alligators, lions, and a gorilla—escaped into the surrounding region. Some elephants, camels, and lions were recovered, while the Bengal tiger, which had immediately begun to hunt nearby livestock, was dispatched by a local bear hunter. But no one's sure where the rest of the animals went, although locals told stories of sighting snakes, parrots, and even a kangaroo for years to come.

**Difficult Tracking**

## Difficult Tracking

The first recording of the Beatles' "Strawberry Fields Forever" was demoed on acoustic guitar by John Lennon, at home. In the studio, he laid the tune down on new tracks, with Paul McCartney adding the flute intro and George Harrison playing slide guitar. During the late-night recording sessions, producer George Martin wrote cello and trumpet arrangements, while the nineteen-year-old engineer, Geoff Emerick, played around with backward masking and Harrison added traces of svarmandal, an Indian instrument. But when Lennon heard the "final" version, he decided he liked the opening bars of his demo better and told the team he wanted the two versions mixed. They weren't played at the same speed. They were different arrangements. They weren't even in the same key. And in that predigital era, the engineer's only tools were scissors and actual magnetic tape. But somehow Martin and Emerick managed to pull it off—and produce one of the masterpieces of the band's career.

## Legendary Lumber

## Sweet Teeth

Thousands of years before the birth of Christ, the Maya people embellished their teeth with gold, turquoise, and jade. For more than a thousand years after that, well-off Japanese people dyed their teeth black as a coming-of-age ritual at puberty and a permanent mark of high status. And all the way back in 1178, Chinese explorers who traversed the Philippine mountains reported meeting a tribe whose members wore gold teeth.

**Things That Are Green**
**Chinese Explorers**

## Chinese Explorers

A hundred years before Europeans reached the Indian Ocean, China had a giant fleet of trading ships, with a crew of almost thirty thousand, counting both fighters and sailors. These "treasure junks" were reported to be five times the size of Christopher Columbus's biggest ship, and were dismissed as legend for generations—until recent excavations of an ancient Chinese shipyard turned up timber masts that matched the legend's specifications.

**Legendary Lumber**

## Legendary Lumber

What makes the legendary Stradivarius violins so great? They're made from the same simple woods—spruce, willow, and maple—used in other stringed instruments, and they have the same contours and angles. But experts around the world swear nothing sounds the same. And when scientists compared Strads with other instruments, they discovered there *was* a difference: the top and bottom panels of Stradivarius violins have remarkably similar density, unlike other instruments whose top and bottom panels have far more variation in density.

**Wild Willows**

## More Than a Maid

Imogene Holmes started out as a maid at George Remus's law office. But after she became Mrs. Remus in 1920 and he became the greatest bootlegger in American history, she presided over a New Year's Eve party where guests found thousand-dollar bills under every plate. But when the first female assistant attorney general of the United States, Mabel Walker Willebrandt, sent a crack Prohibition agent after Remus, the agent fell in love with Imogene, who fell in love with him. Furious, Remus killed Imogene—but was declared not guilty by a sympathetic Cincinnati jury, most of whom had probably enjoyed his wares.

**First Lady**

## First Lady

Mabel Walker Willebrandt became the first female assistant attorney general of the United States shortly after American women got the right to vote in 1919, and just as Prohibition hit in 1920. She wasn't a teetotaler herself, but one of her primary tasks was hunting down bootleggers. She was the one who came up with the idea of charging the crooks income tax on their ill-gotten gains, the strategy used to nab Al Capone in 1931.

**Wait, Prohibition Worked?**
**Mad Skills**
**Successful Bootleggers**

## Things That Are Green
## Wild Willows

When a willow tree feels itself getting nibbled by bugs, it lets out a special warning scent that tells other willows in the area to start growing different leaves—ones that are way harder on the bugs' digestive systems.

**Drinks Made Out of Trees**

## Mad Skills

After Mabel Walker Willebrandt stepped down from her federal office, she went into private practice as an attorney in California, with clients including the actors Clark Gable and Jean Harlow. And she also chose all the furniture at the original Chateau Marmont, the famous hotel still favored by celebrities today, which was built by a friend of hers on Los Angeles's Sunset Boulevard.

**Celebrity Hangouts**

## Successful Bootleggers

Al Capone got famous as a Chicago bootlegger, but he was a New Yorker at heart—he was born in Brooklyn in 1899. He ordered the assassination of seven Windy City rivals on Valentine's Day 1929, but he wasn't apprehended until 1931—for tax evasion.

**What's in This Drink?**

## Wait, Prohibition Worked?

Prohibition is something of a joke these days, but despite the fact that the law was repealed in 1933, after a little more than a decade, it changed American drinking habits forever. Americans drank an unbelievable amount of alcohol in pre-Prohibition days: in 1830, they consumed 7.1 gallons of pure alcohol per person, per year. That's the equivalent of more than three stiff drinks a day—including whiskey for breakfast and lunch, a common pre-Prohibition habit. During and after Prohibition, that rate dropped precipitously. Today, Americans imbibe about one drink per person, per day.

**Laws That Didn't Work**

## What's in This Drink?

What percentage of your drink is pure alcohol, anyway? Depends on what you're drinking. Beer's about 5 percent alcohol, wine about 12 percent, and liquor 40 percent—as the size of a pour goes down, the alcohol content goes up.

**Drinks Made Out of Trees**

## Laws That Didn't Work

In 1974, Richard Nixon pushed through a widely hated national speed limit of 55 miles per hour, mainly to reduce gas consumption but also to improve safety. The unpopular law was repealed in 1995, despite dire warnings from its supporters, who predicted an increase in crashes. But when speed limits jumped, fatalities didn't. Turns out, most people drive pretty safely, no matter the speed limit. And the ones who don't, don't pay much attention to the posted limits, no matter what they are.

**Speed Demons**

## Drinks Made Out of Trees

You know those pretty blue berries you see during the holidays in evergreen wreaths? That's juniper, which is also the key ingredient in gin.

**Sky Blue**

## Speed Demons

Pilots and race car drivers break speed records, but stunt driver Evel Knievel went so fast he actually took flight. His motorcycles, including one powered by a rocket, soared from one ramp to another over lines of cars and trucks, tanks of sharks, and other obstacles. Despite some crashes—including one during an attempt to jump the fountain at Caesars Palace—he managed to survive over seventy-five spectacular public jumps and spent his later years selling his own paintings all over the country, out of the back of his RV.

**Recreational Vehicles**

## Celebrity Hangouts

Today, the Hermitage is a famous Russian art museum, but before it opened to the masses, it was the czar's Winter Palace, and the only people who got to see the art were royalty and their guests—in full evening dress.

**Royal Formalwear**
**Winter Palaces**

## Royal Formalwear

European kings are often depicted in brocade and fur, but at the height of their power in the sixteenth century, rulers of the Ottoman Empire may have worn the most luxurious garments in history, sewn from silk woven with threads of real gold and silver.

**River of Gold**

## Winter Palaces

The Chinese city of Harbin, just south of the Russian border, creates a frozen theme park every winter full of gigantic, beautifully lit ice sculptures of everything from traditional pagodas to ice replicas of Russian churches and the Roman Colosseum. The tradition was started during the Qing dynasty by local fishermen who carved lanterns of ice from the nearby Songhua River and lit them with candles.

**River of Gold**

## Recreational Vehicles

The first motorized RV was produced by Pierce-Arrow in 1910, not even two years after the first Model T rolled off the Ford assembly line. But it wasn't exactly built for the masses: its back seat turned into a bed, but it also featured a telephone to connect to the chauffer, whose own seat folded down into a sink so that you could wash your hands after using the chamber pot.

### Life Before RVs

## Sky Blue

Why is the sky blue? Air molecules in the atmosphere scatter sunlight as it hits them, and blue light vibrates faster than other colors in the spectrum. Since blue light vibrates faster, the air molecules scatter more blue light than other colors—making that big expanse of air we call sky look blue.

### What About Sunsets?

## River of Gold

The California gold rush began in 1848, when carpenter James Wilson Marshall was working to build a sawmill for John Sutter on the American River, at the foot of the Sierra Nevada Mountains. Marshall spied some shiny flakes in the water, and over the next decade, lucky miners pulled over 750,000 pounds of gold from the region.

**Go West!**

## Life Before RVs

Conestoga wagons were first built along Pennsylvania's Conestoga River by Germans who'd immigrated to Lancaster County. They developed the signature arched canvas cover and an ingenious curved floor that kept loads of up to six tons from shifting. The wagons are a fixture in pioneer movies, but in real life they were too heavy to play a part in the long-distance western migration. Instead, they were mostly used to transport goods from rural farms to cities in Pennsylvania, Ohio, Maryland, and Virginia.

**Go West!**

## Go West!

New York newspaper editor Horace Greeley is widely credited with the famous words "Go west, young man, go west!"—an exhortation to migrate across the continent in the service of what he saw as Manifest Destiny. But Greeley himself only ever ventured west once, and only got as far as Colorado, during that state's gold rush, in 1859. Local fans named the town of Greeley after him when it was founded a decade later as a utopian experiment, but even that wasn't enough to induce him to return. Greeley spent most of his life comfortably ensconced in New York City, "pioneering" only as far as Westchester County, a few miles north. In fact, there's no record that he ever really spoke or wrote the famous words, despite his fervent support of western expansion.

**Utopian Experiments**
**Rocky Mountain High**

## What About Sunsets?

At sunset, the angle of the sun means that light has to travel through more of the atmosphere than it does at other times of day to reach a human eye—so a lot of the short blue rays that we see during daylight hours are scattered before the light gets to us. That's why we see the reds, pinks, and oranges on the horizon.

**So Many Sunsets**

## Utopian Experiments

Many of the inventors of early submarines were utopians, hoping to build a better society under the sea, away from the cultures that ruled on land. They weren't trying to invent a machine of war but a technology that might create more peace.

**War Machines**

## Rocky Mountain High

The highest peak in the Rocky Mountains is Mount Elbert. Miners named it in honor of Samuel Hitt Elbert, the Colorado governor who negotiated a treaty with Ute leaders in 1873 to open millions of acres of native land to mining companies.

**Tricky Mining Operations**

## So Many Sunsets

The Mexican painter Diego Rivera lived the last years of his life in Acapulco, at the home of his friend the businesswoman Dolores Olmedo. From her view over the water, he painted twenty-five sunsets. Twenty of them are still on view in Olmedo's Mexico City home, now turned into a major museum of his work.

**Ocean Views**

## Tricky Mining Operations

The toughest miners in the world may be the Indonesian men who harvest sulfur from craters on Mount Ijen, an active volcano on the island of Java. The smell is terrible and the work is dangerous, but they're some of the only people who ever get to see the volcano's blue flames climb the crater walls, or stand on the banks of the crater's poisonous lake.

**Blue Light**
**What Is Sulfur For?**

## What Is Sulfur For?

Sulfur is a key ingredient in sulfuric acid, which humans make more of than any other artificially created chemical in the world. Why? Sulfuric acid is a key ingredient in fertilizer—which ensures that we're able to grow enough food.

**Key Ingredients**

## Blue Light Ocean Views

On Mudhdhoo Island in the Maldives, the surf glows an eerie blue at night, when the motion of the water wakes up bioluminescent plankton.

**Glow in the Dark**

## War Machines

During World War II, the U.S. Office of Strategic Services (which later became the CIA) developed a chemical weapon that smelled like farts. French Resistance fighters were supposed to spray it on German officers, who would then be incapacitated by the wound to their pride. But since the person who sprayed the stuff ended up smelling worse than the target, the idea was abandoned.

**Dangerous Flatulence**

## Glow in the Dark

You can tell different kinds of fireflies apart because every species has its own unique pattern of flashes. And in some places, including mangrove forests in Southeast Asia and the Allegheny National Forest in Pennsylvania, all the fireflies in the area will flash in unison.

**Flashing Lights**

In New Zealand's Waitomo Glowworm Caves, it's not just the worms that glow but the webs they weave: the sticky threads glow in the dark to create a sparkling canopy that lures in dazzled insects.

**Flashing Lights**

Australia's ghost mushrooms give off an eerie green light from under their fleshy tops, not unlike the underlighting of a souped-up hot rod.

**Flashing Lights**

When it senses a threat, the vampire squid, which lives more than 600 feet below the ocean's surface, shoots glow-in-the-dark slime—made out of squid snot.

## Flashing Lights

Most animals that glow in the dark live underwater, especially deep in the ocean, where almost no light penetrates. But on land, there are some insects that light up, including a glow-in-the-dark cockroach, *Luchihormetica luckae*. But don't worry about finding them in your kitchen at night: only one specimen was ever discovered, on a volcano in Ecuador seventy years ago, and scientists worry that the species may have already gone extinct.

## Flashing Lights

## Dangerous Flatulence

You might feel like you'll die if anyone smells your farts—but what will actually hurt you is holding them in. Held captive in your digestive system, gas can damage your intestinal walls and colon.

**Let It Go**

## Key Ingredients

Hershey's chocolate contains a chemical that we can also taste in Parmesan cheese and sour butter: butyric acid. It's what gives the American chocolate its signature tang—but it's also the main scent in vomit.

**Stinky Cheese**

## Flashing Lights

What's the brightest thing an approaching alien would see on Earth, from outer space? The lights of Las Vegas.

**Approaching Aliens**

## Let It Go

In 1986, Cleveland's United Way tried to break a world record by releasing 1.5 million helium balloons into the sky over the city. But officials bumped up the release time to stay ahead of an incoming storm, and after a few glorious moments, the balloons and the storm collided. Under normal conditions, helium balloons deflate before falling to earth, but the change in temperature caused them to drop from the sky, still inflated. Giant piles of errant balloons forced local airport runways to close, snarled traffic, freaked out horses in the surrounding Ohio hills, and even hampered a Coast Guard rescue.

**Freaked-Out Animals**

## Stinky Cheese

Gorgonzola may be one of the world's oldest blue cheeses, appearing in the countryside near Milan sometime around AD 900. Legend has it that blue cheese was created in a lucky accident, when a drunk cheesemaker left a loaf of bread in his cheese cave. Mold grew on the bread, then migrated to the cheese, creating the now-prized blue veins.

**Cheese Origin Stories**

## Cheese Origin Stories

The first cheese in the world, stories say, was invented by an Arab trader who prepared for a journey by pouring milk into a bag fashioned from a sheep's stomach. On his way, rennet from the pouch was heated by the desert sun, and when he opened his bag that evening, he had the honor of sampling the world's first cheese.

**Drinks in Bags**

## Freaked-Out Animals

How do you stop a cattle stampede? Old-time cowboys galloped up in pairs to the front of the herd, then crowded the leader so it started to turn. Once the leader begins to turn, the whole herd will eventually start to run in circles. And to make sure you and your partner know where each other are while you're doing all this—make sure you both sing!

**Running in Circles**

## Approaching Aliens

On a July night in 2001, just after midnight, drivers began to pull off the New Jersey Turnpike to gawk at the sky. Orange and yellow lights had formed a V above the Arthur Kill, a tidal strait between Staten Island and New Jersey. The lights hovered there for almost fifteen minutes before they disappeared, and no official explanation has ever been given.

**Staten Island**

## Running in Circles

Whether they're built for athletes, horses, or race cars, racetracks are oval to give racers a chance to build up momentum on the straightaway before going into the curves that keep them in sight of curious spectators.

**Big Fat Zero**

## Drinks in Bags

Modern connoisseurs might turn their noses up at wine in a bag, but the wineskin—a bag made from animal hide—was one of the earliest methods for storing wine, mentioned as far back as Homer's *Odyssey*. Glass bottles are the upstart: they didn't come on the scene until the 1800s.

**Long Trips**

## Staten Island

The fantasy author George R.R. Martin grew up in Bayonne, New Jersey, in sight of Staten Island, New York City's oft-forgotten fifth borough—and the island's shape was the inspiration for his fictional land of Westeros.

**Fictional Lands**

## Long Trips

When Odysseus finished fighting the Trojan War, he was only about 565 miles from his home in Ithaca, on the west coast of ancient Greece. But his beef with Poseidon, god of the sea, made his travels literally epic. After tangles with a Cyclops and some Sirens, and a brief stint in the Land of the Dead, it took him ten years and almost 5,200 miles at sea to get back home. But his biggest delay wasn't caused by any of the monsters he had to best—it was the seven years he spent under the spell of the nymph Calypso and her beautiful singing.

**Land of the Dead**

# Big Fat Zero

What's the most important number in math? It might just be zero. Because ancient Greeks, Romans, and Egyptians didn't have it, they weren't able to calculate very large numbers or do algebra, algorithms, or calculus. Europeans only began to use zero during the Moorish conquest of Spain, when it arrived with Arab traders who had learned it in India, where the number first originated. But zero also appeared one other place: in the Maya calendar, although the Maya people never used it in equations.

**Bad Math**

# Long Trips

Birds are famous for migrating because we see them squawking overhead on their seasonal flights north and south. But deer, bugs, fish, and even snakes migrate as well. The world champion mammal migrator is the humpback whale, which has been known to migrate 6,000 miles.

**Massive Migrations**

## Fictional Lands

The Homestead Act of 1862 was signed by Abraham Lincoln to encourage Americans to move west. But the government wasn't the only one handing out land: railroads and other private companies bought up huge tracts, to resell at a profit, then advertised them with outlandish and sometimes outright false promises, including describing the Plains state of Nebraska, admitted to the Union in 1867, as "the Garden of the West." But when homesteaders tried farming techniques that worked out east on the new land, many stripped away soil-preserving grasses and almost immediately created dust-bowl conditions on their new farms.

**Long Trips to Fictional Lands**

## Land of the Dead

California's Death Valley is known as one of the harshest climates in the world. With recorded temperatures as high as 134 degrees Fahrenheit, almost nothing grows there. But about once a decade, heavy winter rains wake up long-buried flower seeds, filling the Death Valley desert with a surprise ocean of blooms.

**Surprise Ocean**

# Massive Migrations

Monarch butterflies migrate almost 2,000 miles, but they live only two to six weeks. So no single monarch butterfly ever makes it through a round-trip migration.

## Long Trips to Fictional Lands

Dragonflies double the migration distance of the humpback whale, covering up to 12,000 miles, with help from the wind. And like monarchs, no single dragonfly does the whole run—four generations will live out their lives during the course of one round-trip migration.

## Long Trips to Fictional Lands

Salmon never forget home—and when the time comes for them to spawn, they'll travel almost 2,000 miles to get back there, swimming upstream from the Pacific Ocean, returning to the river where they were born.

## Long Trips to Fictional Lands

## Surprise Ocean

During the Pleistocene Ice Age, northern Washington State was covered with ice that blocked off rivers and lakes, sometimes for centuries. When those ice dams finally broke, seas of water poured into eastern Washington, creating rocky tracts of land that still have virtually no soil.

**Crazy Waterways**

## Long Trips to Fictional Lands

In the age of exploration, mapmakers would place dots on maps where they had heard there might *possibly* be an island. Sometimes the islands were really there, and sometimes they were based on false reports, or sightings of flotsam, ocean creatures, or even other ships. It didn't matter all that much— unless you were a shipwrecked sailor trying to decide which route to take home with limited resources.

**Crazy Waterways**

## Bad Math

The June 2000 grand opening of London's Millennium Bridge, a suspension footbridge over the river Thames, only lasted half an hour, after multiple people were knocked off their feet by its bucking. The culprit: Designers had worked in 2D, neglecting to correct for side-to-side motion. Total repair bill: $9 million.

**Crazy Waterways**

## Crazy Waterways

Florida's Seven Mile Bridge is actually a few tenths of a mile shy of 7 miles, but it spans an impressive and beautiful stretch between Marathon Key and Key West, with the Florida Bay to the north and the Atlantic Ocean to the south. A modern road has replaced the original railroad bridge, an epic project built by Henry Morrison Flagler, who served as John D. Rockefeller's henchman in building Standard Oil and then turned his attention to the opening of Florida, building a railroad through the new state and profiting by increased land values all along the route. But when his railroad got to its planned last stop at Miami, Flagler, already sixty-five, decided that wasn't far enough. Despite the miles of open ocean between Miami and Key West, and the swampy bottom in the shallows below the waves, he insisted that the railroad would go all the way through to the final key. The project took him more than a decade to complete and cost millions of dollars—and over a hundred lives, when a 1906 hurricane hit workers mid-construction. Flagler was eighty-two when he finally stepped out of his private train car in Key West, after taking his inaugural trip on his railroad across the ocean. He didn't live to see his railroad tracks swept away by an even bigger hurricane, in 1935.

## Hard-to-Build Railroads

# Hard-to-Build Railroads

When it came time to build the first transcontinental railroad, the U.S. government didn't pick just one contractor: the Pacific Railroad Act anointed two separate companies, the Union Pacific and the Central Pacific, to start building from opposite directions. The Central Pacific started in Sacramento, California, and the Union Pacific started in Omaha, Nebraska, which was then the end limit of the country's existing railroad networks. Both companies got $48,000 and thousands of acres of land for every mile built—so speed was key to collecting. But the Central Pacific had to blast through the Sierra Nevada mountain range before it could start building the simpler straightaways that the Union Pacific enjoyed immediately outside Omaha. In the first months of building, the Union Pacific laid four times as much track as the Central Pacific. But once the Central Pacific broke free of the Sierra Nevada, its teams of largely Chinese workers, in prime shape because of the fight through the mountains, quickly made up for lost time, beating the competition mile for mile for much of the ensuing build. The final tally two years later, in May 1869, when the two companies grudgingly agreed to meet on Utah's Promontory Summit: 690 miles for the Central Pacific, and 1,086 for the Union Pacific, which added up to a very patriotic 1,776 miles.

**Big Rocks**

# Big Rocks

Europeans who streamed into Egypt during the colonial period were fascinated by hieroglyphs on ancient walls, but not even modern Egyptians could read them until the discovery of the Rosetta Stone in 1799. A helpful ancient bureaucrat had decided that the same decree be carved into a single stone in three languages: ancient Greek, and two previously unreadable Egyptian scripts. Since modern scholars could still read ancient Greek, they were able to begin to decipher the ancient Egyptian scripts as well. But what did the stone actually say? Carved just after Ptolemy V ascended to the throne, it was issued by priests giving orders for how the new ruler should be worshipped, including praise of his gifts to the people of Egypt and plans for celebrations of his birthday. The only thing that's different in the different languages is a handful of dates—maybe because someone was hoping either the Greeks or the Egyptians would show up on the wrong day for the party.

**Weird Rocks**
**Secret Languages**
**Birthday Parties**

## Weird Rocks

A hunk of orpiment might seem like a tempting meal, because it gives off a faint smell of garlic. But the scent comes from high levels of arsenic in the rock, which ancient Chinese used as a coating for poison arrows.

**Poison Arrows** ━━━━

## Secret Languages

Secret societies sometimes communicate in codes, and some, like the Masons, even develop their own languages. But the most secret languages of all are the ones only two people speak, created by twins because of the rare accident of having another person around all the time who is at exactly your same stage of language development. About 50 percent of all twins, whether they're fraternal or identical, develop their own private language, known as cryptophasia.

**Infamous Twins** ━━━━
**Who Speaks Secret Languages?** ━━━━

## Poison Arrows

According to Homer, poison arrows were used by both sides in the Trojan War. Medical texts in China and India describe poison weapons in use as early as 500 BC. And some Native Americans used poisons on the tips of both arrows and spears. But poison arrows weren't the only form of old-time biological warfare: ancient soldiers also threw wasp's nests over enemy walls, filled bombs with scorpions, and sent flaming pigs scuttling through the ranks of their enemies.

**Angry Insects**
**Delicious Bacon**

## Birthday Parties

Some scholars say that a biblical mention of the Egyptian pharaoh's birthday was the first recorded birthday party, although others think the reference probably refers to his coronation day, when he was believed to have been "born" into godhood. Romans were the first culture to celebrate the birthdays of regular Joes—although only the Joes, because Roman women didn't get birthday parties. Fiftieth birthdays were an especially big deal for Romans, celebrated with a honey, cheese, and olive oil cake.

**Did Someone Say Birthday Cake?**

## Who Speaks Secret Languages?

The word *cant* refers to highly developed collections of slang that almost operate as their own language, usually used by people who don't want the whole world knowing their business. Polari is a good example: it was developed in England in the 1800s by a gay community that wanted to avoid detection. In Polari, *drag* meant "clothes"—which is where we get the modern term *drag queens.*

**Keeping Secrets**

Think it's hard to decipher an English accent? English thieves in the 1500s developed something even more incomprehensible, on purpose, because they didn't want anyone who overheard their nefarious plans to understand what they were saying. The slang was called Thieves' Cant, and you probably speak some today if you've ever used the words *sham*, *rascal*, *shoplift*, *swag*, or *slang*—which is what the Thieves' Cant called itself.

**Keeping Secrets**

The French language has also been known to produce cant, most notably Verlan, in which French words are broken into pieces, then inverted. Nineteenth-century prisoners used it to keep jailers from understanding their conversations. Starting in the 1970s, Verlan was introduced to the general population by rappers, and became common parlance among French youth in the 1980s. Its name is actually an example of Verlan, which takes the French word for "reverse," *l'envers*, and turns it inside out.

**Keeping Secrets**

Klingons aren't real, but their language is. An actual linguist created it for the *Star Trek* television show, then wrote several books on the vocabulary and grammar—enough that you can learn to speak it yourself, and keep up on your skills by subscribing to the quarterly journal published by the Klingon Language Institute.

**Keeping Secrets**

## Did Someone Say Birthday Cake?

Germans were the first to make what modern people would recognize as birthday cake, in the late 1700s, as part of children's birthday celebrations that also featured blowing out one candle for every year a child had been alive.

**What About Wedding Cake?**

## Infamous Twins

What's scarier than the Godfather? Twin Godfathers! For almost twenty years, starting in the early 1950s, identical twins Ronnie and Reggie Kray ruled the underworld of London's East End, involved in everything from protection rackets to murder while mingling with celebrities in city clubs. The tide turned against them after they brutally murdered a member of their own gang who had failed to complete a hit job. Spooked, other gang members started to talk to authorities for the first time, and the twins were sentenced to life in prison in 1969.

**Hitsville History**

## Delicious Bacon

What was the first meal someone ate on the moon? Unless little green people snacked on something we don't know about, it was bacon. Buzz Aldrin and Neil Armstrong enjoyed the savory strips along with peaches, coffee, and sugar cookies shortly after the July 1969 landing—the kind of breakfast kids might choose when they're a good 238,900 miles away from Mom.

**Bacon Bugs**

## What About Wedding Cake?

When England's Queen Victoria married Prince Albert in 1840, it was the first time an English queen who was currently on the throne had gotten married in three hundred years. The young couple celebrated with a wedding cake that weighed three hundred pounds, spread over three tiers, with busts of the two of them adorning the top—which set off a craze for wedding cakes throughout England and eventually around the globe.

**Motown Weddings**

## Motown Weddings

Smokey Robinson married his fellow Miracle Claudette Rogers, while early star Mary Wells married one of the company's original backup singers, Herman Griffin. Berry Gordy's sister Anna married Marvin Gaye, while his sister Gwen married singer and producer Harvey Fuqua. And the writing team of Nickolas Ashford and Valerie Simpson, who penned "Ain't No Mountain High Enough" and "Ain't Nothing Like the Real Thing" married each other in 1974—and stayed together until Ashford's death in 2011.

**Not a Hit**

## Hitsville History

Hitsville U.S.A. is the name that the record executive Berry Gordy put up on the face of Motown Studios not long after he opened the label in Detroit in 1959, from a recording studio in the basement of a family home.

**Not a Hit**

An unknown Marvin Gaye played drums on the Marvelettes' 1961 hit single "Please Mr. Postman."

**Not a Hit**

The same musicians played on virtually every record Motown made during the 1960s, including James Jamerson, Benny Benjamin, Johnny Griffith, Robert White, Joe Hunter, Joe Messina, Jack Ashford, Richard "Popcorn" Wylie, and bandleader Earl Van Dyke, collectively known as the Funk Brothers. But it wasn't until Marvin Gaye's "What's Going On" was released in 1971 that any of their names ever appeared on a Motown album.

**Not a Hit**

Paul Williams of the Temptations made up the signature talk-to-the-hand dance move for the 1965 song "Stop! In the Name of Love" and taught it to Diana Ross as they were rehearsing for a BBC special.

**Not a Hit**

David Ruffin imagined he was singing to his daughter when he recorded the vocal to "My Girl."

**Dumas's Dad**

# Keeping Secrets

Alexandre Dumas's novel *The Man in the Iron Mask* isn't merely a fictional invention: Louis XIV really did confine a man for thirty-four years, during which time the prisoner wore an iron mask, softened by a velvet cloth, over his face. Two musketeers reportedly watched him at all times, not to guard him from harm but to kill him if he ever tried to remove the mask. Even after the masked man's death, in 1703, the secret didn't come out. Louis XIV's men destroyed his clothes, furniture, and other personal items, and melted down the mask itself. Theories abound on the man's identity—including one by Voltaire, who speculated that he was the half brother of Louis XIV, while in Dumas's epic tale, the prisoner is the king's younger twin, and a threat to his throne. Others suggested he was Louis XIV's true father—which would mean that Louis XIV was not the son of a king and therefore shouldn't sit on the throne himself. The man was also rumored to be a general, a valet, and even the illegitimate son of an English king. But Louis XIV and his loyal musketeers managed to keep this secret for all of history, even after their own deaths. Today, nobody has any proof of the identity of the unfortunate captive.

## Dumas's Dad

## Angry Insects

Young Charles Darwin was an inveterate bug collector. One day, he'd scooped up two fine specimens, one in each hand, when he found a third he simply had to have. Since he didn't have a third hand, he popped it in his mouth, where the angry bug promptly spewed a noxious fluid, causing Darwin to spit it out.

**Bacon Bugs**

## Not a Hit

When Johann Sebastian Bach conducted the world premiere of his *St. Matthew Passion* on Good Friday in 1729, most of the people in his hometown of Leipzig weren't there. They'd all gone to see a passion written by Christoph Gottlieb Fröber, who people in the know thought was the Next Big Thing. After a few more performances in Bach's lifetime, his passion wasn't played again until Felix Mendelssohn revived it in 1829. But today, it's considered by many to be the greatest piece of music ever written.

**Also-Rans**

## Dumas's Dad

Alexandre Dumas's father, Thomas-Alexandre Dumas, was born in Saint-Domingue (now Haiti) to an enslaved woman of African descent and a French nobleman, and rose to become a general under Napoleon. He is credited with incredible feats of strength and bravery, including picking up a horse from the ground with his legs while hanging from a tree by his hands, and defending a bridge against an entire troop of enemy soldiers by himself. But Napoleon came to hate him, probably out of jealousy, and allowed him to languish for years as a prisoner of war in the Italian town of Taranto. While Thomas-Alexandre's wife pleaded with officials to bring him home, his health was destroyed by imprisonment. Napoleon refused to grant him a pension upon his release, and he died at age forty-three, just a few years after returning home. He was one of the only people of African heritage ever to lead a European army, but today he's the only one of Napoleon's generals who doesn't have his own statue in France.

## Horse Tricks

## Bacon Bugs

What do you do when screwworms have infested your skin? One real, contemporary modern medical intervention is to place bacon on the affected area. The stuff is so much more delicious than anything else, including us humans, that the parasites can't resist it—and crawl out of our skin to nosh.

**Favorite Foods**

## Horse Tricks

In the first decade of the 1900s, a German math teacher gained worldwide notoriety with the claim that he'd taught his horse, Clever Hans, to do math. Public interest was so intense that the German government appointed a thirteen-person panel to investigate. Their finding: Hans couldn't count, but he was really, really good at reading faces. In answer to a problem, he'd keep tapping his hoof until he could tell from the expression of the listener that he'd arrived at the right answer.

**Large Panels**

## Also-Rans

New York senator Rufus King, a signer of the Constitution, was an antislavery Federalist who ran for president in 1816 but lost by a huge margin to John Madison as the Federalist Party was crumbling: he got about one electoral vote per five for Madison.

**Bad Parties Thrown by Corrupt Politicians**

Republican James Blaine lost the presidency in 1888, perhaps because of a taste for questionable railroad deals, which looked especially sketchy in a race against anticorruption crusader Grover Cleveland.

**Bad Parties Thrown by Corrupt Politicians**

Preacher William Jennings Bryan, at thirty-six, was the youngest person ever nominated for president. As the Democratic nominee in 1896, he faced fierce opposition: all the major papers urged their readers to vote for William McKinley, his opponent. But Bryan made speeches to five million people in the course of his campaign and earned 47 percent of the popular vote. And when FDR introduced the New Deal four decades later, people complained that it sounded just like what Bryan would have wanted.

**Bad Parties Thrown by Corrupt Politicians**

Eugene V. Debs lost the race for president in 1920, which isn't completely surprising, since he was in jail at the time. The labor leader had been locked up on charges of espionage for his antiwar stance, but he still pulled a million votes in the general election, at a time when only about a hundred million people lived in the United States.

**Bad Parties Thrown by Corrupt Politicians**

Democrat George McGovern is still famous for his epic loss to Richard Nixon in 1972, after Nixon did some dirty dealing to make sure he got to run against McGovern instead of Edmund Muskie, who was considered more electable. McGovern lost by more than 20 percent of the popular vote. But his candidacy reshaped the Democratic Party.

**Bad Parties Thrown by Corrupt Politicians**

Alf Landon was a contender for U.S. president in 1936, even though virtually no one today knows his name. The incumbent, Franklin Delano Roosevelt, obliterated him—winning the electoral college vote 523 to 8—perhaps due to Landon's lackadaisical campaigning style: he didn't make a single campaign appearance for two full months after his nomination.

**Guys Named Landon**

## Favorite Foods

Napoleon rose to power from relative obscurity, and he never lost his taste for simple fare. His favorite foods were potato soup or beans with onions, and he liked to soak up the juices from his plate with a piece of bread. That's when he ate at all—the little emperor was also famous for skipping meals.

**Napoleon's Height**

## Large Panels

Hieronymus Bosch's *The Garden of Earthly Delights* is painted on three wood panels, about 7 feet high and 13 feet wide, total. At the time he painted it, in the early 1500s, oil on wood was cutting-edge technology: oil paint had been invented less than a century before. And when you close the two sides of the triptych, there's another painting on the opposite side, in shades of gray, depicting a glass globe that encloses the whole world.

**Glass Globes**

# Napoleon's Height

Everyone's heard that Napoleon was short, but he was probably five foot six—pretty normal for a guy born in 1769. The confusion may have arisen from a difference between French and English measurements in his autopsy, but it may also have been an extremely successful piece of English propaganda.

**Tricky Autopsies**

# Favorite Foods

The Big Mac wasn't invented by McDonald's corporate but by a Pennsylvania franchisee, Jim "MJ" Delligatti, who dubbed it the "Big Attraction." McDonald's owner Ray Kroc took it nationwide in 1968, a year after Delligatti dreamed it up.

**Inventive Italians**

# Inventive Italians

Leonardo da Vinci was born out of wedlock, to an Italian lawyer and a peasant girl, then raised on his father's estate until he was around fifteen, when he was sent away to apprentice with a sculptor. He had virtually no formal education.

**Surviving Sculptures**

## Surviving Sculptures

Nobody's sure if any sculptures by Leonardo still exist, although some scholars claim a figure of a smiling Mary holding a laughing child Jesus, housed in London's Victoria and Albert Museum, is his only surviving work in 3D.

**Survival of the Biggest**

## Survival of the Biggest

Leonardo may or may not have made the smiling Madonna, but one statue of his was finally completed almost five hundred years after his death, from plans he first drew in 1482 for a bronze horse that would weigh 15 tons and stand 25 feet tall. He managed to construct a 24-foot clay model for the birthday of his patron's daughter, but when war broke out, all the metal in the area was cast into weapons, and his plans were scrapped. Modern art patron Charles Dent got interested in following Leonardo's plans in 1977, but it wasn't until 1999, five years after Dent's death, that Nina Akamu, a Japanese American sculptor, finally completed Leonardo's sculpture, now on display in Milan, Italy, with an identical replica in Michigan.

**Master Plan**

## Master Plan

Leonardo hated the idea of war, but he worked for the military to make a living. He designed the first parachute and the first armored tank, along with diving gear, a flying machine, robotic armor, and a compound gun that shot off rounds from eleven muskets in succession. Many of them were never produced, but in modern times, several projects have made his original plans reality, including the British Army's build of his armored fighting vehicle. Modern engineers had to tweak the design of his gears, which didn't quite work in reality, but some scholars have suggested that Leonardo's flub with the mechanics might have been deliberate—a way for him to give the appearance of aiding the military without really building working war machines.

### Judging By Appearances

## Judging By Appearances

Apparently, Leonardo was a hottie. Multiple contemporary reports describe him as being incredibly physically attractive, with long hair that curled all the way to the middle of his back and a signature pink tunic.

### Laws of Attraction

## Bad Parties Thrown by Corrupt Politicians

Nero probably didn't set Rome on fire. But after fires ravaged the city, he was terrified that the people might riot over the rumors that he had. So he decided to throw a party in his gardens for all of Rome's finest, but his choice of lighting didn't exactly prove that he wasn't a vicious pyromaniac. To illuminate the nighttime festivities, he had prisoners, including Christians, tied to stakes and set on fire.

**Scary Gardens**

## Guys Named Landon

Michael Landon was famous as Pa on the television series *Little House on the Prairie*, and he warmed hearts later in his career in *Highway to Heaven*. Born Eugene Maurice Orowitz, he picked "Landon" out of a phone book, guessing, probably accurately, that it would be more conducive to Hollywood fame. His famous chestnut mane started graying in his twenties, so he resorted to dyeing his hair himself, until the cheap dyes started showing up purple on film, and he turned to a professional for help.

**Little House on the Prairie**

## Glass Globes

The invention of the snow globe was an accident: Erwin Perzy, an Austrian mechanic, was tinkering for ways to increase the brightness of early light bulbs. He was trying to imitate a trick shoemakers used to make their candles more powerful: refracting their light through a globe of glass, filled with water, so they could do detailed work into the night. One day, he picked up a handful of semolina and dumped it in one of his experimental globes—and realized it looked just like falling snow as it sank. Not long after, he added figurines to the watery scene, and the snow globe was born. For the first forty years, his globes always depicted the same thing: a tiny snowbound church.

**Underwater Church**

## Little House on the Prairie

The descriptions of life on the frontier in *Little House on the Prairie* and other books in the series by Laura Ingalls Wilder make you feel like you can see everything she's describing—perhaps because Laura's fourteen-year-old sister, Mary, lost her sight to a viral illness and their parents told Laura, just twelve years old at the time, that from then on she needed to be Mary's eyes. So for the next six years, until she married and moved away, Laura described everything happening in the world around them to Mary, in great detail.

**Books About Girls**

## Books About Girls

Louisa May Alcott had no desire to write *Little Women*. The former Civil War nurse wanted to publish a book of short stories, but her publisher wanted a story for girls and promised to publish her father's philosophy manuscript, too, if she turned one in.

**Civil War Nurses**

Alcott wrote a dozen chapters of *Little Women* in a matter of weeks, drawing from her own childhood. She thought the result was boring, and so did her publisher—but her publisher's niece and several other young girls loved it, so Alcott pressed on, churning out the final draft in ten weeks, "in record time for money," she wrote. It was published four months after she started writing.

**Record Time**

Alcott's previous novels, published under the name A. M. Barnard, featured cross-dressers, espionage, and drugs.

**Noms de Plume**

Alcott's childhood home was a stop on the Underground Railroad, where her family sheltered people escaping from slavery.

**Great Escapes**

A suffragist, Alcott was the first woman to register to vote in Concord, Massachusetts, in 1879, when women were given the vote in local elections.

**Early Suffragists**

## Scary Gardens

The English love to garden, but the planters at Alnwick Castle in Northumberland might love it to death. Among the other formal gardens outside the castle, Alnwick's Poison Garden contains over a hundred plants that are deadly, used in drugs, or might make you drunk, including common but poisonous plants like laurel hedge, opium, and hemlock. The favorite plant of the duchess who created the garden in 1996: angel's trumpet, which works as a powerful aphrodisiac—right before it kills you.

**Tricky Autopsies**

## Underwater Church

The Temple of Santiago was built in Chiapas, Mexico, in 1564 by Spanish monks, including the friar Bartolomé de las Casas, who spoke out against slavery in the New World. The monks thought the area would one day be a great city, but the church was abandoned after a plague hit in the eighteenth century. In 1966, the church was submerged under a hundred feet of water by the construction of the Nezahualcoyotl Reservoir, arches and all. But in recent years, droughts have been so extreme that the reservoir has dried up, and until the rains returned, visitors could walk through the old temple for the first time in decades.

## Buried Temples

# Buried Temples

The giant cathedral that graces the central plaza in Mexico City isn't the only house of worship that has ever stood there. It was built on the foundations of an Aztec temple. Those ancient foundations remain solid, but the church above them is sinking into the surrounding land. One part has settled a full 8 feet more than the rest, and a crack has opened down the center of the building. But Mexican engineers invented a solution to stabilize the cathedral—and possibly other leaning buildings, like the famous tower in Pisa.

**I Want Pizza**

# Noms de Plume

Samuel Clemens took his pen name, "Mark Twain," from Mississippi River jargon. Mary Ann Evans took the name George Eliot in hopes of being taken more seriously—just like the Brontë sisters, who published as Currer, Acton, and Ellis Bell, and fooled contemporary critics into arguing that no woman could write like them. But the Chilean poet who began life as Ricardo Eliécer Neftalí Reyes Basoalto took the name Pablo Neruda because his father disapproved of his writing.

**Disgruntled Dads**

## Early Suffragists

Women began to demand the right to vote in the mid-1800s. Suffragists staged demonstrations and hunger strikes in the United States, while their compatriots in the United Kingdom did everything from running onto the racetrack to throw the king's horse off course at the 1913 Epsom Derby, to bombing major public sites, including the National Gallery and Westminster Abbey. American women got the right to vote through a constitutional amendment in 1920. Full suffrage for all Englishwomen came in 1928. But New Zealand beat them both, welcoming women to the polls in 1893.

**I Want Pizza**

## Record Time

The Beatles had been playing clubs in Liverpool and Germany for years before they made it big, so when they went in the studio to record their first full-length album, they knew exactly what to do. They'd already recorded four singles that had been hits, but they laid down the final ten tracks for *Please Please Me* in just thirteen hours.

**A Taste of Honey**

## Tricky Autopsies

In 1533, a pair of conjoined twins, the infants Joana and Melchiora Ballestero, died on the island of Hispaniola, and the Catholic Church decided to do an autopsy, not because there had been any signs of foul play, but to answer a theological question: Did they share a soul? Remarkably, the officials actually came to a conclusion: because the twins had two hearts, they must have two souls. The theologians may have been pleased to come to a scientific conclusion, but it was the twins' father who had to face the most practical consequence: he had to pay for two baptisms.

**Disgruntled Dads**

## Civil War Nurses

Before he became one of America's most famous poets, Walt Whitman was a Civil War nurse. In the very first battle he served in, Fredericksburg, he found his own wounded brother. Whitman grew to be so trusted by Union doctors that he was put in charge of a whole trainload of wounded men bound for hospitals in Washington, and he put his skills as an author to work for them, writing messages to their loved ones.

**War on Birds**

## I Want Pizza

Fussy eaters aren't always trying to be jerks—some of them suffer from a genuine condition that makes it very difficult for them to tolerate certain tastes and textures. One food almost all of them can enjoy, according to a recent study by Duke University: pizza.

## A Taste of Honey

## Laws of Attraction

If you think someone's stolen your spouse's heart, you can sue them for financial damages in seven states: Illinois, North Carolina, South Dakota, New Mexico, Mississippi, Utah, and Hawaii. But that isn't the weirdest law about relationships still on the books. In Mississippi, you're not allowed to get a marriage license when you're drunk, and in Kentucky, you can marry the same person three times—but not four. And in the small Massachusetts town of Truro, men have to prove their virility by killing six crows or three blackbirds before tying the knot.

## War on Birds

## Disgruntled Dads

When St. Francis of Assisi gave up his partying ways and got interested in rebuilding the crumbling churches of his day, he funded his charity by selling goods that belonged to his father, a powerful cloth merchant, without permission. Furious, his dad dragged him into court, demanding repayment. Francis stripped down to his skivvies, left the clothes his dad had bought him behind, and walked out into the hills around Assisi, singing.

**Saints Alive!**

## A Taste of Honey

Beekeepers in Brooklyn couldn't figure out why the bees in their rooftop beehives had suddenly started to produce honey that was almost Day-Glo red—until they realized that the maraschino cherry factory in the neighborhood had left the top off their enormous vats of sticky red syrup, which the bees had started harvesting just like sweet nectar from a flower.

**Up in the Air**
**Maraschino Cherries**

## Saints Alive!

Legend has it that in the third century, St. Denis of Paris was beheaded by the Roman governor, THEN carried his own head six miles from the place of his execution to Montmartre, resting place of the French kings, and later home of a thriving bohemian arts scene.

**Broke Artists**

When St. Margaret of Antioch was thrown into a Roman prison for refusing to get married, the story goes, Satan turned up in her cell in the form of a dragon and promptly ate her. But Margaret was holding a cross, which she used to cut her way out of his stomach.

**Tough Girls**

Whenever Joseph of Cupertino thought about God, he floated up off the ground. He did it in front of his fellow monks, and in front of the pope. Sometimes he'd pick his buddies up and float around with them. The crowds who came to see him levitate during mass became such a problem that the church locked him up. Every now and then they'd check to see if he could celebrate mass without levitating, but he couldn't stop himself—so he spent his entire life confined.

**Up in the Air**

Some people think that saints are something more than human—but St. Guinefort was an actual dog. Legend has it that his owner left him with the baby while he went out to hunt. When he got home, he found no sign of the baby but saw the dog covered with blood, so he killed the animal in a rage. But when the baby began to cry from under the bed, the man realized that his loyal pet had saved the baby by killing a snake. Ever since, the home of the brave pup has been a pilgrimage site.

**Dogs Are Awesome**

Quitera, Marina, and Liberata were three of nine second-century Portuguese sisters born at the same time to the same mom. Their mom was embarrassed to have given birth to nonuplets, and even more disappointed that they were all girls, so she told her maid to drown them. But the kindly maid hid them in a distant village, where they grew up to form a gang that broke Christians out of jail. When Roman police captured them, they were returned to their father, who tried to marry them all off. But they escaped and continued to stage guerrilla attacks against the Roman Empire until all of them were killed—and Quitera, Marina, and Liberata became saints.

**Tough Girls**

## War on Birds

In 1932, the Australian Army went to war with a bunch of flightless, 80-pound birds. The Emu War was fought against twenty thousand emus who refused to decamp from land the government had set aside for veterans who were trying to farm it. The giant birds were destroying crops, and when the former soldiers asked for help, the Australian Army sent in the artillery. They used everything from heavy guns to trucks to pursue the birds, but for months, the emus distinctly had the upper hand: in one sortie, 2,500 rounds of ammunition were spent nabbing only two hundred birds. Finally, the army came up with a solution the veterans had been asking for all along—providing them with enough ammo to run the birds off themselves.

**Up in the Air**

## Broke Artists

Legend has it that whenever Pablo Picasso stopped in at the Montmartre eatery Au Lapin Agile, he paid for lunch with a drawing.

**Bar Food**

## Great Escapes

John Gerard, son of an English nobleman, became a Jesuit priest in England during the reign of Elizabeth, when it was a crime to be a Catholic. He pretended to be a fashionable gambler but worked in secret to encourage English Catholics, until he was locked up in the Tower of London, where authorities tried to torture him into giving up his friends. Instead, Gerard chiseled through the stone around his cell door and snuck past his captors to a tower wall high above the moat. Several stories below, a friend threw him a rope. Gerard secured it to a nearby cannon, threw the other end back to his friend on the opposite bank, and effectively zip-lined to freedom. He was never recaptured.

**Up in the Air**

# Maraschino Cherries

The maraschino cherries you're used to seeing on the top of an ice-cream sundae are actually a knockoff: the originals are called marasca cherries, made from a rare breed of sour cherry and soaked in a premium liqueur developed by the Luxardo family. The bright red version that most of us know was developed, perhaps unsurprisingly, by an American, Ernest Wiegand, who soaked ordinary cherries in a cheaper and sweeter liquid and added the almond flavoring most people now associate with the word *maraschino*.

**Bar Food**

## Up in the Air

In 2013, an illusionist known as Dynamo traveled across London by bus—except that he rode *outside* the double-decker with his hand on the roof, unsupported by anything else as he soared high above the passing traffic. Magic-watchers guessed correctly that he accomplished the trick with the help of an iron bar hidden in a fake arm, but the jury is still out on how Dynamo accomplished other tricks, including walking on water across the river Thames and commanding paper butterflies to come to life.

**Paper Flowers**

## Bar Food

Tired of the same old peanuts and fried pickles? You might be tempted to try Rocky Mountain oysters, served throughout the United States and Canada. But read the ingredients first: the deep-fried snacks aren't actually oysters, but the testicles of pigs, sheep, or bulls. Think you'd rather try something more like China's drunken shrimp? They're exactly what they sound like. The only catch? They're still alive.

**Unusual Oysters**

## Tough Girls
## Paper Flowers

Mary Delaney was the daughter of a noble English family that had fallen on such hard times that they married her off while she was still a teenager to a rich old drunk who ran around on her and flaunted the fact that he wasn't leaving anything to her in his will, which was made out to his children from an earlier marriage. One night, he came home intoxicated and told her that he wanted to make his will out to her. She told him to wait til morning, but he died before daybreak. Penniless, she lived alone until her forties, when she met a curate who was brilliant and penniless like her, but already married to a rich woman. Years later, after his wife's death, he showed up on Mary's doorstep and they enjoyed such a joyful marriage that Mary thought she might die of grief when he passed away. Instead, at age seventy-two, she started to make remarkable, botanically correct images of flowers using decoupage: cutting scraps of hand-painted paper and pasting them to black cards. The king of England heard about her project and began to provide her with botanical specimens, and by the time of her death, at eighty-eight, she had created almost one thousand delicate works of art, which she said she saw as praise to God for the beauty of creation, and which remain a beloved treasure of the British Museum today.

**Things Kings Collect** ━━━━━━━━━━━━━━━━━

## Dogs Are Awesome

The average dog can learn about 250 words—around as many as the average two-year-old human "puppy."

**Cats Are Awful**

Big dogs are smarter: research shows that large dogs remember things longer than small ones do.

**Cats Are Awful**

But border collies are the smartest of all: they can learn commands in about five seconds—and remember them 95 percent of the time.

**Cats Are Awful**

Dogs can read. Multiple dogs have been trained to recognize commands written on cards and respond to them—even when the words are in different fonts.

**Cats Are Awful**

Dogs can tell if you're scared or sad, based on chemical changes in your scent. And some have been known to detect cancer before medical tests revealed it, or even notice if family members are pregnant—before they start to show!

**Changes in Your Scent**

Dogs don't just love you for the food. When they're separated from a human companion they've bonded with, many will exhibit signs of grief—including losing their appetite or refusing to eat. And it's not just their humans they miss: dogs show grief when they lose their furry friends, like other dogs—or even cats!

## Cats Are Awful

The good people of Cormorant, Minnesota, elected a Great Pyrenees named Duke as their mayor in 2014. He served four consecutive terms before going to Dog Heaven in 2019.

## Accomplished Dukes

When the planes struck the Twin Towers on September 11, 2001, Roselle, a guide dog for the blind, was already at work on the seventy-eighth floor with her owner, Michael Hingson. Despite the noise and panic around them, Roselle, a yellow Lab, safely guided Hingson down 1,463 steps, leading him outside to safety just before the building fell. Ever heard of a cat doing anything like that?

## Hero Cats

## Things Kings Collect

The Russian royal family was known for their collection of Fabergé eggs, which contained hidden treasures like tiny elephants ridden by even tinier men, lilies of the valley made from pearls, and even a working model of a carriage made almost entirely from gold. But Prince Frederick of Brandenburg may have had the craziest collection of all: he collected giants. Five foot three himself, Frederick, who later became the king of Prussia, recruited a military regiment composed entirely of men six foot two and taller, who came to be known as the Potsdam Giants. The regiment eventually grew to 3,200 strong, and the king himself led them through daily drills and trotted them out to impress foreign visitors. When he was feeling sick or blue, he made them process before him, following a live bear, their regimental mascot, and he was known to paint the portraits of many of the giants, from memory.

**Unusual Eggs**
**Painted by Memory**

## Accomplished Dukes

Duke Ellington was such a towering figure in American music that the president of the United States threw him his seventieth birthday party. Richard Nixon invited Ellington to the White House to celebrate, along with jazz legends Dizzy Gillespie, Benny Goodman, and Earl Hines—who started to jam together after the official program wrapped up. But it wasn't the first time a member of Ellington's family had been to the White House: his father, James Edward Ellington, who gave Duke his first name, Edward, served as a butler in the White House during the Harding administration.

**Jam Sessions**

## Unusual Oysters

When the first Dutch arrived in New York harbor in the mid-seventeenth century, they found oysters the size of dinner plates.

**Setting the Table**

## Changes in Your Scent

Europeans were late to the party with perfume: Persian, African, and Arab cultures all had a rich tradition of scent creation long before Europeans got interested in perfume in the 1300s. Italians were the first Europeans to make scent in earnest, perhaps because Venice was a center of trade that brought oils and spices from the East. Catherine de' Medici introduced perfume, bottled in beautiful Murano glass, to France. Curious what those original Medici perfumes were like? The company that created the scent for Catherine's wedding is still in business—and still produces her bridal fragrance, from its original recipe.

**Persian Perfumes**

## Jam Sessions

Jam was probably made for the first time in the Middle East, where sugarcane is a native plant. The first recipe for jam appears in the first known cookbook, written in Rome in the first century. But jam didn't become popular in the rest of Europe until it was brought back by knights returning from the Crusades.

**Lies About Jam**

## Persian Perfumes

Persians were some of the first perfumers in the world, and scents mattered so much to Persian royalty that kings often had their own signature scents—which were off-limits for their friends and relatives to wear. Western perfuming owes so much to Persians that the word *rose* can be traced back to the original Persian, which influenced ancient Greek, Latin, and French.

**Old Roses**

## Lies About Jam

Scottish legend has it that marmalade was created by the Scots in Dundee sometime around 1790, after a ship full of oranges wrecked on the coast.

**The Truth About Jam**

## Unusual Eggs

Horn shark egg cases are about 5 inches long, shiny black, and shaped so much like a corkscrew that you might be able to drill wood with them—if you needed a fastener that size.

**Choosing Caviar**

## The Truth About Jam

One of the earliest mentions of marmalade in a cookbook was made by an Englishwoman, Elizabeth Rainbow, wife of Bishop Rainbow of Carlisle. She included a recipe for orange marmalade as part of a cookbook she wrote in the 1680s—more than a hundred years before the Scottish claim they invented it.

**Controversial Rainbows**

## Painted by Memory

Vincent van Gogh's *Starry Night* is one of his most famous paintings, and perhaps one of the most famous paintings in the world. It depicts the view from the asylum where he was confined after cutting off his ear. He was still in the sanatorium when he painted it, but it was painted from memory—he re-created the vivid nighttime scene during daylight hours. And it omits one crucial detail: the bars on the windows to his room.

**Prison Roses**

## Old Roses

Fossil evidence shows that roses may have been blooming on earth 35 million years ago. Since then, they've proliferated across the entire Northern Hemisphere, but it was the Chinese who probably began to domesticate them, almost five thousand years ago. Prized everywhere for their beauty, roses are valued so highly that they have been accepted in trade and barter as legal tender for centuries, all over the world.

**Prison Roses**

## Choosing Caviar

Russian and Persian fishermen were the first to collect caviar, from the Caspian Sea. The tiny fish eggs have been considered a delicacy since the time of ancient Greece, and they've even been prescribed as an antidote for depression. How do you pick the good stuff? Hold a can of packed caviar up to your ear. The sound of the eggs bumping together should sound like a cat's purr!

**Canned Goods**

## Controversial Rainbows

The Greek poet Homer seemed to think that all rainbows were purple, perhaps because he was famously blind. Aristotle insisted there were three colors, and during the Renaissance, the palette was expanded to four: red, yellow, blue, and green. Isaac Newton's calculations came up with seven colors, adding violet, orange, and indigo—but modern China names just five. Maybe that's because rainbows are really an optical illusion. No two people see the same rainbow. Because we all have slightly different eyes, and all see from different perspectives, we each see our very own.

**Shifts in Perspective**

## Prison Roses

Charles E. Chapin was a high-powered New York newspaper editor but wound up in financial ruin. Filled with shame, he killed his wife, Nellie, rather than tell her the truth about their situation, and was sent to Sing Sing, where he became famous for turning the prison grounds into lush rose gardens.

**Sing Sing**

## Shifts in Perspective

The ceiling of Grand Central Terminal is a beautiful turquoise, decorated with constellations—but a few weeks after it opened, a stargazing commuter pointed out that it was backward: east was west. That's actually because the map reversed when it was projected by painters—but some people joke that it's a God's-eye view of the world, looking down through the stars.

**Troublesome Ceilings**

## Sing Sing

The name of one of America's oldest prisons, opened in 1828 on the Hudson River in upstate New York, comes from a Native American tribe, the Sintsinck, whose name translates loosely as "stone against stone."

**Lost in Translation**

## Cats Are Awful

Tiger roars are so powerful that they've been known to paralyze any animal within range—including human trainers—perhaps because they're capable of roaring at frequencies that are below human hearing but still affect our bodies. Or perhaps because they're just so darn loud.

**Things We Can't Hear**

## Hero Cats

Gary Rosheisen trained his cat, Tommy, to call 911, because Rosheisen knew he might one day be incapacitated by his medical challenges, which included minor strokes and osteoporosis. But Rosheisen was never sure what Tommy was capable of until a seizure caused Rosheisen to fall from his wheelchair in December 2006. Just as Tommy had been trained, he went to the phone and dialed with his paws. When emergency responders arrived, they found the only human in the place unable to move, and couldn't figure out who had called them—until they realized it was the hero cat.

**Amazing Wheelchairs**

## Things We Can't Hear

What animal has the best hearing on earth? Most of us have seen a dog react to sounds beyond the range of human hearing, but the animal that hears at the most extreme frequency yet measured is a moth. Why does it need to hear at 300 kilohertz (a level astronomically beyond the range of human hearing, which detects sounds between 20 hertz and 20 kilohertz)? Perhaps because bats, their natural predators, make sounds in exactly that range.

**Going Batty**

## Amazing Wheelchairs

British citizen Jim Starr was tired of not being able to go off-road in his wheelchair, so he decided to design one whose special treads can take him over mud, snow, or even the beach. He designed it hoping it'd let him spend more time outside with his wife and kids, but the British version of the DMV has told him he can only use it on private land—because it's so big that, by law, it qualifies as a tank.

**A Day at the Beach**

## Going Batty

Each spring, Bracken Cave outside San Antonio becomes home to an estimated twenty million bats, who migrate there to give birth to their "pups." As many as five hundred of the baby bats can hang from a single square foot of cave ceiling, which helps them boost each other's body heat. But the cave's gigantic bat population, almost four times the number of people in New York City, is a fraction of the total bat population worldwide. Bats make up one-fifth of all mammals on earth—and they're the only mammals that can fly.

**Troublesome Ceilings**

## Lost in Translation

One of the most memorable moments of the Cold War between the United States and the Soviet Union came when Soviet premier Nikita Khrushchev began to bang a shoe on his desk before the United Nations in 1960. And many Americans today can quote his language at the time: "We will bury you!"—terrifying words from one of the world's great nuclear powers to another. Turns out, that was a sloppy translation. The meaning of the Russian wasn't nearly as threatening—more along the lines of "We'll still be here when you're gone."

**Khrushchev's Third Shoe**

## Troublesome Ceilings

In Mexico's Yucatán Peninsula, some members of a species of red-and-yellow snakes that usually subsist on rats have started to literally crawl the walls of local caves, building homes in nooks in the cave ceilings. They do it because it gives them access to a whole new kind of food—bats. When the bats that share the cave fly in or out, the snakes emerge from their holes and dangle upside down in the dark, snacking on bats they snatch out of the air.

**Snakeskin Shoes**

## Khrushchev's Third Shoe

Perhaps the oddest part about Khrushchev's shoe banging at the United Nations was that, according to several contemporary sources, he was still wearing two shoes *while he banged a third*, which may suggest he hadn't lost his temper so much as planned a very carefully calculated bit of theater.

**Snakeskin Shoes**

# Canned Goods

Canned food wasn't invented to help out desperate housewives—the process was created by a French chef, during Napoleon's rule, to provide a stable source of food for the French army and navy as they rampaged through Europe and beyond, stretching their supply lines to the breaking point. Around 1803, young Nicolas Appert, from the region of Champagne, came up with the idea of jamming fresh food into airtight containers, which in his case were champagne bottles. But within a few years, Appert had switched to jars with wider mouths, then began to experiment with preserving meat in tins. But can openers weren't invented for almost another thirty years—because until then, soldiers just used their bayonets to slice off the tops.

**Inventions for Napoleon**

## Setting the Table

The original meaning of *set the table* was pretty literal: in medieval days, people actually set up movable tables by laying a big board across a pair of braces, and guests brought their own utensils with them, even to feasts thrown by royalty. And in those days, even royalty didn't eat off plates, but piled their food on slices of bread, laid directly on the makeshift tables. Over time, as manufacturing expanded, hosts began to collect their own silverware, plates, and glassware, displayed in ever-increasing complexity. By the Victorian era, a "proper" table setting required about twenty pieces per guest. And in case that wasn't enough to impress their company, the elite began to create more and more elaborate centerpieces, including one English aristocrat who decorated his table with a working silver fountain filled with live fish. With the explosion in manufacturing during the Industrial Revolution, the average family was able to buy their own "silverware" (even if it wasn't made of silver), but left behind much of the complexity of Victorian settings, leaving us with what you're likely to find when you sit down at any restaurant with table service: knife, fork, and spoon.

## Superstitions About Silverware

## Snakeskin Shoes

Snakeskin shoes are the height of modern fashion, for both women and men, with price tags running easily into the thousands. But back in the 1930s, in the heart of the Great Depression, snakeskin became popular as a thrifty solution to the fact that most people couldn't afford real leather. Designers started to use snakeskin, along with lizard and crocodile, because it was an inexpensive alternative.

**Thrifty Designers**

## Inventions for Napoleon

Before radio and smartphones, soldiers who wanted to communicate with each other at night had a tricky problem: how to read a message in the dark without giving away their position by the flare of a light. For Charles Barbier, a French soldier under Napoleon, the problem was personal: he'd seen several men killed when they lit lamps at night in order to read a message. He solved this problem by developing "night writing," a code composed of raised dots on paper. Sound familiar? That's because another inventive Frenchman, Louis Braille, simplified Barbier's night writing into a code that could be read with a single touch of the human hand—and eventually spread around the world as a language for people with limited vision.

**Night Vision**

## A Day at the Beach

The longest beach in the world stretches 150 miles: Brazil's Praia do Cassino, or Casino Beach. Its white sand spreads farther than the entire coastlines of Georgia, New York, or New Jersey. In second place: New Zealand's informatively named Ninety Mile Beach. The only problem with it? Huge waves make it too dangerous to swim there, so it's actually used as a public highway when nearby roads are closed—and visitors bodyboard the sand dunes but avoid the surf.

**Crazy Casinos**

## Thrifty Designers

Things were so tight for the average family during the Great Depression that women started to make their clothes out of fabric they got for free: the bags that held feed for farm animals. So feed companies hired designers from New York and Europe to create feed bags with style, hoping they'd be more competitive if their fabrics were on-trend.

**Hungry Horses**

## Night Vision

Owls have great night vision—perhaps because some of them have eyes so big they take up over half the space in their skull. But their eyes are so big that they can't move them as much as humans can, which is why owls can turn their heads a full 270 degrees.

**Vision Problems**

Cats can get up to all kinds of tricks at night because they see better than we can in the dark. They need about a tenth of the light humans do to see clearly, because they have eight times as many rods per cones in their eyes as we do.

**Hot Rods**

Snakes have something called thermal vision, which means they can actually *see* body heat—even in the dark.

**Body Heat**

Night-vision goggles show the world in green because the human eye is most sensitive to that color.

**Get Some Glasses**

Henry Fuseli's *The Nightmare* is one of the most famous paintings in the world, showing a grim demon sitting on top of a sleeping woman clothed in white. And it may have been an influence on Mary Shelley's classic *Frankenstein*: the author's mother, the early feminist Mary Wollstonecraft, had a youthful crush on Fuseli, and Mary Shelley knew the artist as a family friend to both her mother and her father, William Godwin.

**Artistic Vision**

## Hungry Horses

Pigs get a bad name because they used to serve as agricultural trash compactors, eating all the garbage on a farm. But horses, though they strongly prefer to graze, will sometimes eat odd things like wood shavings, sand, the tails or manes of other horses, and manure—if they're bored or underfed.

**Expensive Crap**

## Superstitions About Silverware

Knives have probably been used to help us eat ever since they were invented, and spoons date back to shells that people once used to scoop up edible liquids, like broth. But forks are relative newcomers on the utensil scene, probably first used by Persian nobles in the eighth and ninth centuries. As a result, they've been the subject of some strange superstitions. In the eleventh century, the Byzantine saint Peter Damian thought using a fork was a criminal form of luxury: when a noblewoman who ate using a golden utensil made of two tines died of the plague, Damian considered it just punishment for the indulgence of using a fork. Fork use migrated to Italy, then entered wide use in Europe in the sixteenth century, introduced (along with ice cream!) by Catherine de' Medici after her marriage to England's Henry II. But people still thought of forks as frivolous and unnecessary for centuries, even into the late nineteenth century, when British soldiers refused to use them on the grounds that it was unmanly.

## The Invention of Ice Cream

## Hot Rods

NASCAR didn't exactly start as a gentleman's sport, like Europe's tonier sports car races did. The American stock car racers have their roots in Prohibition, when bootleggers revved up standard autos with supercharged engines so they could give the feds the slip while transporting their illegal cargo. Southern bootleggers started racing their souped-up vehicles before Prohibition even ended—and when it did, the races continued, with the first official NASCAR race held at Daytona Beach the day after Valentine's Day 1948. And the winner of that first race, Red Byron, had earned his skills back in the day, delivering contraband moonshine.

**Big Races**

## Body Heat

The Pompeii worm makes its home near ocean vents that pour out hot water from undersea volcanoes, and can tolerate the highest temperatures of any multicelled animal: over 176 degrees Fahrenheit.

**Cold Blooded**

## Artistic Vision

Auguste Renoir, the famous impressionist, may have been more of a realist than anyone realized: his blurry paintings may have reflected his profound near-sightedness, which meant that the blurred landscapes that made him famous were pretty much all he could see.

**Get Some Glasses**

Self-portraits by Rembrandt van Rijn, the Dutch master, show his eyes pointing slightly outward. This could have meant he lacked depth perception—but it could also have given him an advantage as an artist, helping him see things his peers with more straightforward vision might have missed.

**Dutch Stuff**

Pablo Picasso's paintings might make you dizzy because of his genius—or because he didn't have depth perception, because the alignment of his eyes was unusual. But he didn't see it as a drawback—in fact, he thought it made it easier for him to create on canvas: a 2D world.

**Feeling Dizzy**

## Get Some Glasses

Glasses cost about two hundred bucks, on average, but the materials used to make them are worth a couple of bucks at most. So why are they so expensive? One Italian company, Luxottica, owns most of the major prestige eyeglass brands—and most of the world's eyeglass stores. With a worldwide monopoly, it can charge pretty much whatever it wants.

**Monopoly Money**

## Feeling Dizzy

Jazz great John Birks "Dizzy" Gillespie was one of the architects of bebop, a major force in introducing Cuban jazz to the United States, and an inspiration for Miles Davis. But how did he get his nickname? The young Gillespie was full of humor and mischief, which led his bandmates to give him a name in keeping with his onstage antics.

**Cuban Improvisation**

## Crazy Casinos

Probably the most famous piece of casino trivia in the world is the rumor that casinos pump oxygen onto their floors to keep people alert and playing. It's not true, and it would actually be a crime if it were. So why do so many people believe it? Probably because of a Mario Puzo novel, *Fools Die*, which features a fictional oxygen-pumping casino, Xanadu.

**Lucky Breaks**

American roulette wheels are different from European roulette wheels, which have one less zero slot than American wheels do. What's that mean for players? American wheels give the house a more significant advantage.

**Lucky Breaks**

The big moneymakers in casinos aren't the high-stakes games. Slot machines bring in the most cash. But the first slot machine wasn't installed in a casino. A San Francisco mechanic named Charles Fey invented it to entertain customers waiting for their cars.

**Lucky Breaks**

Citizens of Monaco aren't allowed to gamble in the tiny nation's world-renowned Monte Carlo Casino. But they do get a pretty good consolation prize: no one in the country has to pay taxes because of all the money foreigners drop at their gambling tables.

**Tiny Nations**

FedEx was about to go bust in 1973, until company owner Frederick Smith flew to Vegas and won $27,000 at the blackjack tables—giving the company enough cash to stay afloat until it finally turned a profit for the first time in 1976.

**Lucky Breaks**

## Expensive Crap

One of the most important imports to nineteenth-century America was guano, otherwise known as bird poop. The droppings of seabirds, full of fish protein and condensed when dried by the sun, are a fantastic fertilizer, and on the islands off Peru, where guano was first "mined," it sometimes stood as much as 200 feet deep. When shippers started to import it into the United States in the 1830s to help replenish fields stripped by farming, guano provoked an agricultural boom and proved to be such a cash cow that explorers fanned out across the oceans, hunting for similar fortunes of poop. Mining guano was dangerous and toxic, done mostly by indentured servants from China. And it was dangerous and unpleasant cargo, because of the distance of transport and the stink. But it was so important to the U.S. economy that President Millard Fillmore urged Peru to lower the high prices it had set on its bird poop, and the United States passed the Guano Islands Act, allowing the government to annex any unclaimed islands with guano deposits, in order to take advantage of the treasured poop.

### Unclaimed Islands

## Big Races

Lance Armstrong wasn't the first cyclist to cheat for a win. In 1904, the second year of the Tour de France, some cyclists faced roads strewn with glass and nails, or got beat up by the fans of rival riders. Others hopped trains or automobiles to get ahead. Twenty-seven people finished, but twelve of them were disqualified—including everyone in the top four.

**Bad Roads**

## Cold Blooded

Alaskan wood frogs hold the record for enduring the coldest temperatures, for the longest period: they can live for almost seven months at an average temperature of 6 degrees Fahrenheit.

**Frozen Stuff**

## Monopoly Money

The famous board game Monopoly is usually played as a gleeful celebration of capitalism in which every player tries to grab as much as they can. But the original inventor, a progressive feminist named Elizabeth Magie, actually created it to teach players about the practical consequences of rich landlords squeezing everything they could from the regular guy.

**Land Grabs**

# Frozen Stuff
# The Invention of Ice Cream

Nobody's sure who invented ice cream, but it definitely dates back to ancient days. Alexander the Great is on record as having eaten a delicacy composed of snow, honey, and flavoring from flowers. And the infamous Roman emperor Nero sent servants up into the mountains to collect snow, which he ate mixed with fruit juice.

**Alexander the Great**

Marco Polo brought a recipe for something like sherbet back with him from his travels in Asia, which likely provided the basis for all Italian gelato. But English royalty may have invented ice cream for themselves as well. Charles I, in particular, was quite fond of a dessert he called "cream ice."

**Marco Polo**

George Washington owned not one but two pewter ice-cream pots, and is recorded to have spent $200 on ice cream in a single summer in 1790. Adjusted for today's rates, that's about five thousand bucks.

**Stuff George Washington Liked**

No one but the rich could afford ice cream until around 1800, when ice houses were invented, allowing the average family to keep things cool year-round. In 1851, a dairyman from Baltimore, Jacob Fussell, started the first manufacturing of ice cream on a large scale.

**Ice Land**

Sundaes were originally called Sundays—and served on Sunday, to ward off the accusation that ice-cream sodas, made from ice cream, syrup, and seltzer water, were so decadent they were sinful. In response, soda fountains left the fizzy soda out on Sunday—and a whole different kind of treat was born: the gooey mix of ice cream and topping that's still a favorite today.

**Sins of Omission**

Today, Americans enjoy more than 1.6 billion gallons of ice cream every year: about the size of a water tower for a midsize city.

**Water Towers**

## Dutch Stuff

The world's biggest tulip festival isn't in the Netherlands, but in Canada. It started just after World War II, when the Dutch royal family gifted tulips as thanks for Canada's role in sheltering them during the war. The festival features over a hundred kinds of tulips—and over a million blooms.

**Big Bouquets**

## Unclaimed Islands
## Tiny Nations

In the English city of Portsmouth, the three small islands that dot the surface of Baffins Pond caught the attention of local teacher Louis Robert Harold Stephens. A bit of research turned up the fact that the little scraps of land were not mentioned in the contract when the original owner sold the land to the government as a park. So Stephens named them the Lagoan Isles—and proclaimed himself grand duke.

**Land Grabs**

## Cuban Improvisation

Under the U.S. embargo of Cuba, which began in 1960, Cubans could no longer purchase Coca-Cola—so they invented a homegrown variety, TropiCola, which got so popular it actually became one of the country's exports.

**Surprising Exports**

## Vision Problems

Helen Keller became the first deaf and blind person to earn a college degree, and gained worldwide fame as she fought for women's rights, worker's rights, and peace. But none of it might have happened without her teacher, Anne Sullivan. Visually impaired herself, Sullivan was only twenty when she took on the task of educating the seven-year-old Keller. She taught Keller to speak, read, and write, and stayed with her for decades, until Sullivan's death.

**Reading Lessons**

## Marco Polo

Nobody knows how pool tag got the name Marco Polo, but it first appeared in the United States in the 1960s, perhaps spurred by the wide availability of swimming pools. It's nothing like water polo, much more like a watery version of Blindman's Bluff, which people have played on land since the 1500s.

**So Many Swimming Pools**

## Bad Roads

Until 1921, the United States had no general plan for building roads. But with the advent of the automobile, Congress passed an act that required states to plan highways with the federal government. The system was finished in breathtaking time: by 1923, the new roads served 90 percent of the country.

**Freeway Firsts**

## Alexander the Great

Alexander the Great conquered vast swaths of the ancient world, from Macedonia to India. Along the way, he founded over seventy cities, all of which he named Alexandria, after himself—except for Bucephala, named after his favorite horse, Bucephalus, who died in the battle to claim it.

**Land Grabs**

## Freeway Firsts

The first mile of concrete highway anywhere in the United States was built in 1909, just outside Detroit, the Motor City, between Six and Seven Mile Roads.

**Motor City**

## Lucky Breaks

Ludger Sylbaris survived a volcanic eruption on Martinique in 1902—because he'd been thrown in jail for drunkeness. The stone structure protected him when the volcano exploded the next morning, and wiped out the entire town. He started life afresh as "The Man Who Lived Through Doomsday," with the Barnum & Bailey Circus.

**Greatest Show on Earth**

## Water Towers

Most water towers contain approximately a day's worth of water for the surrounding town: about fifty times more water than the average swimming pool. But the structures have also turned into giant local art projects. The one in Gaffeny, South Carolina, is painted to look like a peach. In Ellsworth, Illnois, the water tank looks like a gigantic baseball. And outside Disney Studios in Hollywood, the water tower sports mouse ears.

**So Many Swimming Pools**

## Motor City
## Surprising Exports

Before Detroit became the automotive capital of the world, the city was the world's biggest exporter of cast iron stoves. The city's expertise in metalwork and engineering was what positioned it to become a powerhouse producer of cars.

**Heavy Metal**

## Land Grabs

Oklahoma, which means "Red Man's Land" in Choctaw, was the last major piece of land owned by Native Americans after the forced relocations between 1830 and 1850, known as the Trail of Tears. But in 1889, Congress opened Oklahoma to settlement. Settlers lined up on the borders of the territory, a gun was shot at noon, and they raced to claim the best property. "Sooners" were the settlers who snuck in early to steal the best land—that's who the football team is named after.

**Guns at Noon**

## Ice Land
## So Many Swimming Pools

Some people call Iceland's Blue Lagoon a wonder of the world: a bowl made of lava and filled with water heated by the still-active geothermal forces below. It seems like an ancient feature of the land, and maybe one that far predates human habitation, but the water isn't a natural phenomenon—it's runoff from a nearby geothermal power plant.

**Power Plants**

## Heavy Metal
## Sins of Omission

When Led Zeppelin released its fourth album, with the monster hit "Stairway to Heaven," the album cover didn't show a picture of the band, the band's name, or even a title. Studio executives at Atlantic were furious. But the band members weren't trying to prank their label, or their fans: they were reacting to critics who accused them of putting hype over music. So, Led Zeppelin offered the public nothing *but* music—and the album went on to become one of the most successful in history.

**Stairway to Heaven**

## Reading Lessons

McGuffey Readers were the runaway best sellers of nineteenth-century America, read more widely than any other book except the Bible. William McGuffey, who learned to read from his mother during his childhood in Ohio, wrote the books after Harriet Beecher Stowe (author of another best seller, *Uncle Tom's Cabin*) recommended him to a publisher. His fee for the first two was just $1,000, although the books went on to become the textbook of choice in thirty-seven states.

**Runaway Best Sellers**

## Stairway to Heaven

The Loretto Chapel in Santa Fe, New Mexico, boasts a staircase with a double 360-degree turn and no central support, with all the weight of the structure resting on the bottom step. Built without metal, it's held together by wooden pegs and was constructed by a mysterious carpenter who disappeared as soon as it was complete, giving rise to the legend that it was built by Joseph, the father of Jesus and the patron saint of carpenters.

**Crazy Carpentry**

## Power Plants

Ninety percent of the ethanol in America comes from corn, because it's already a well-established crop. But switchgrass, which covers the Great Plains, can produce far more ethanol: over a thousand gallons per acre. It also needs less water and pesticides, and comes back every year, producing five times as much energy as it takes to grow.

**The Great Plains**

## Big Bouquets

In 1890, Pasadena decided to show off all the local flowers that bloomed there, even in the dead of winter. Citizens covered their horse-drawn buggies with blooms, and the Rose Parade—held annually on New Year's Day ever since—was born.

### Is This Paradise?

In Xochimilco, Mexico City, locals live amid fifty miles of canals, plied by large, shaded, open-sided boats. Each bears a vivid painting with a woman's name. But years ago, those beautiful nameplates were made from fresh flowers, replaced daily.

### Crazy Canals

In the main lobby of New York City's Metropolitan Museum of Art are towering displays of fresh flowers, taller than you are. They're funded by a trust that was established in 1970 by Lila Acheson Wallace, who inherited the *Reader's Digest* fortune. She wanted to make sure that the large architectural pots they stand in were always full, to welcome visitors as they crossed the threshold.

### The Condensed Version

# Stuff George Washington Liked

George Washington received French hounds from the Marquis de Lafayette, bred them with Virginia dogs—the genesis of the American foxhound—and gave them names like Trulove, Drunkard, Singer, and Sweet Lips.

**Favorite Drunkards**

George Washington loved being a farmer. His spread was comprised of 3,000 acres, mostly planted with tobacco, but also included the young country's largest whiskey distillery.

**Alcohol, Tobacco, and Firearms**

Washington loved theater so much that when Congress banned it during the Revolutionary War, he made his own troops perform for him anyway: they put on a play called *Cato*, about a soldier who stood up to a Roman emperor.

**Problematic Soldiers**

Washington never got beyond primary school in his formal education, but he loved books: his library contained 1,200 of them, on everything from military strategy to agricultural lore.

**Beloved Libraries**

## Is This Paradise?
### Crazy Canals

From the time of Cyrus the Great, Persian kings planted "paradise gardens," with a fountain in the center and four canals crisscrossing the plantings, filled with all kinds of flowers and fruits. Their prowess at gardening was said to rival their prowess at war, and they were known to collect fruit trees and exotic creatures on their military campaigns, to enrich their gardens when they returned home.

**Weird Loot**

## Favorite Drunkards
### Problematic Soldiers

According to contemporary accounts, Cleopatra was a heavy drinker, which was actually part of her job as a leader of the cult of Dionysus, the god of drink. But Cleopatra didn't just imbibe: bathing in wine was one of her beauty secrets. Her beauty was so persuasive that Roman general Mark Antony ditched the Roman Army to stay with her. During one of their trysts, she bet him that she could spend a small fortune on a single meal, and won by dissolving a precious pearl in wine before she drank it.

**Collecting Pearls**

## Guns at Noon
## Alcohol, Tobacco, and Firearms

Western movies love the idea of a shootout at noon, but in real life in the Wild West, it almost never happened that way: shootouts came much later in the day, usually after one or both participants had had plenty of time to have their judgment impaired by getting liquored up.

**Eastern Movies**

## Beloved Libraries
## The Condensed Version

Behind St. Peter's Basilica, in Vatican City, are 52 miles of underground bookshelves that condense much of the world's knowledge in the Vatican library. It includes trial records for the Knights Templar, correspondence between the Vatican and Michelangelo—and a hidden section that no outside visitor is allowed to enter.

**Weird Nights**

## The Great Plains

Before the arrival of Europeans in the Americas, the grasslands of the Great Plains were the most prevalent kind of vegetation on the continent, covering far more land than American forests or deserts. The uncut grasses often grew taller than the top of a grown man's head, and riders sometimes stood on the backs of their horses to get a better look at where they were headed.

**Horse Tricks**

## Weird Nights

In the continental United States, the days get shorter during winter and longer during summer. But far to the north, in Alaska and Russia, the summer days get *really* long: between May and July, the sun never sets. That means human residents can party all night—but it also gives plants a round-the-clock growing cycle, which means that some Alaskan plants grow to wild sizes, with 100-pound cabbages, 50-pound cantaloupes, and pumpkins that top out at over 1,000 pounds.

**Russian Summers**

## Crazy Carpentry

After her husband's death in 1881, Sarah Winchester inherited the fortune her husband had made selling rifles, then spent a good chunk of it employing a full-time team of carpenters on the endless project of building her home in San Jose, California. But she was the de facto architect: the team worked so fast to do her bidding that they didn't use blueprints. It's not clear if some of the stranger aspects of the house, including stained glass placed at waist level, and stairs that lead up to blind walls, were mistakes or deliberate decisions. But the resulting structure, which had 160 rooms and was still unfinished at Sarah Winchester's own death, was so strange that a legend developed that Winchester created all the odd spaces to confuse the ghosts of people who had been killed by her husband's rifles.

## Energetic Architects

## Collecting Pearls

Humans have been collecting pearls for at least five thousand years—from the waters around Japan to Scottish rivers, where one of the world's most perfect pearls was found. But pearl diving on a large scale began in Australia, where divers, spurred by worldwide demand, sometimes swam 100 feet below the surface to collect as many mollusks as they could before their single breath ran out. And the biggest pearls are found in the Philippines, where the world's largest, at 75 pounds, was discovered in a giant clam.

**Big Jewelry**

## Russian Summers

St. Petersburg, in Russia, is built on more than a hundred islands, now fused into a single city by over three hundred bridges, and fill. Even though the city's latitude is only two degrees off Anchorage, Alaska, it boasts "beach clubs," where members gather to enjoy the water during fleeting summer months. The city's Florida namesake, St. Petersburg, boasts beaches that are far closer to the equator than the original—along with 361 days of sun a year, and the world record for the most consecutive days of sunshine: 768 in a row.

**Doppelgängers**

# Weird Loot

The golden age of piracy didn't last very long: from approximately 1700 to 1725, when the world's great navies were in their infancies, before they'd brought law to the high seas. Despite popular images of chests full of gold, most pirate loot came in other forms. Pirates weren't above stealing food and booze from their victims, and since they couldn't go to regular shipyards for repairs, they frequently robbed materials from other ships to fix their own. Cannons, gunpowder, and basic tools and medicine were also hard for pirates to get their hands on—so highly prized. But their real haul came from robbing goods being transported by ships they attacked, including spices, cocoa, animal skins, and sugar. To unload the hot merchandise, they sold it at a discount at ports in Jamaica and the Bahamas, where merchants didn't ask too many questions. Some pirates really did amass huge fortunes, including the infamous Captain William Kidd. Part of his buried treasure was dug up on a small island off the coast of New York shortly after Kidd was captured in 1699, but fortune hunters are still searching for more—on the coast of exotic New Jersey.

**Kidding Around**

## Greatest Show on Earth

There's no record of P. T. Barnum ever saying "There's a sucker born every minute." What he did say was "The American people love to be humbugged."

**Bah! Humbug!**

Before Barnum started his famous circus, he founded a museum of oddities, including a working model of Niagara Falls, and the Feejee Mermaid, constructed by fastening a monkey's body to a fish tail. He also managed a huge nationwide tour for the famous singer Jenny Lind.

**Bah! Humbug!**

P. T. Barnum's memoir, published when he was just forty-five, explained in great detail how he'd duped the American people. The public outcry after its publication was vigorous—but that didn't keep Barnum from going on to serve as mayor of Bridgeport, Connecticut, and in the Connecticut legislature, where he fought for the rights of people who had recently been emancipated from slavery.

**Bah! Humbug!**

At age sixty-four, Barnum came out of retirement with the opening of his Monster Classical and Geological Hippodrome in New York City, where he showed off animals and acts that he'd traveled the world to collect, along with an aquarium and modern-day chariot races.

**Bah! Humbug!**

After P. T. Barnum partnered with James A. Bailey in 1881 and they took their show on the road, Barnum's New York City property, transformed into an urban garden by George Gilmore, eventually wound up in the hands of the Vanderbilt family—who opened the original Madison Square Garden on the site: Madison between Twenty-Sixth and Twenty-Seventh.

**Bah! Humbug!**

## Runaway Best Sellers

One of the best-selling single books of all time is a tale of a little boy on a tiny planet with a talking rose: *The Little Prince*, by Antoine de Saint-Exupéry, which has sold 142 million copies since its publication in 1943. But Saint-Exupéry didn't live to see his worldwide fame. In 1944, while flying a reconnaissance mission to collect intelligence about the movement of German troops in the last days of World War II, he vanished without a trace—until an ID tag with his name washed up on the coast near Marseille in 1998.

**Disappearing Acts**

## Bah! Humbug! Doppelgängers

Christmas masses and some Christmas carols date all the way back to the early days of the church. But many treasured modern Christmas traditions were actually invented by Charles Dickens in his 1843 novella, *A Christmas Carol*—including the phrase *Merry Christmas!* Dickens's Ghost of Christmas Present wears a fur-trimmed velvet robe that sounds a lot like what we now think of as Santa's garb, but with one big difference: Dickens's ghost wears green, while Santa's suit is red.

**Old St. Nick**

## Energetic Architects

Senenmut was an ancient Egyptian commoner who rose to become a favorite of Hatshepsut, one of Egypt's rare female pharaohs. Together, they oversaw an ambitious program of building, including a mortuary temple on the banks of the Nile and lavish tombs for Hatshepsut, Senenmut's parents, and Senenmut. His tomb includes the first known star map in Egypt, although he apparently was never laid to rest there. Images of Hatshepsut, powerful in her own time, were systematically erased from buildings and records after her death, but the building projects she and Senenmut created together remain some of the world's most remarkable architecture.

**Star Maps**

## Eastern Movies

Most Americans think of Hollywood as the film capital of the world—but more people on the planet see Bollywood movies, made in India—by a huge margin. Bollywood sells twice as many tickets as Hollywood per year.

**Treasures of India**

## Disappearing Acts

Aviator Amelia Earhart is famous for disappearing over the Pacific in 1937, just shy of her fortieth birthday. But before she became a world-renowned pilot, she served as a social worker in Boston, where she helped recent immigrants settle into their new lives. After gaining notoriety as a pilot, she flew across the Atlantic alone in record time in May 1932, just twelve years after her first ride in an airplane—and debuted a clothing line for active women.

**Memorable Women**

## Big Jewelry
## Treasures of India

India is one of the world's biggest exporters of precious gems, second only to Hong Kong. But unlike some other jewelry markets, Indian culture isn't enamored with diamonds—Indian jewelers are more likely to work with pearls, rubies, garnets, sapphires, or emeralds. The country's love affair with gems dates back centuries, and may have reached its peak when Emperor Shah Jahan covered the Taj Mahal with gemstones in the 1600s.

**Diamonds Are a Girl's Best Friend**

## Old St. Nick

Modern Santa Claus is credited with climbing down chimneys to fill children's stockings with gifts—perhaps the world's most cumbersome way to make a simple delivery. But the tradition stems from a story about the original St. Nicholas, who lived in the fourth century in what is now Turkey. When he heard about a poor family without enough money to give their three daughters a dowry—which left them in danger of a life of poverty or prostitution—Nicholas tossed bags of money through the windows and chimney of their house, so they could marry.

**Chimney Hijinks**

## Star Maps

People were making maps of the stars before they made maps of the earth. The first known star maps were made by astronomers in Babylon before 1100 BC. But the oldest surviving map of land, discovered in Iraq, dates to between 500 and 700 BC.

**Ambitious Astronomers**

## Horse Tricks

After Europeans introduced horses to the Americas, the Comanche people became great riders, using their skills in horsemanship to dominate large swaths of the Southwest. No Comanche was considered a warrior until he could shoot arrows accurately at an enemy while hanging alongside his horse's flank, using the horse as a shield.

**Wild, Wild West**

## Ambitious Astronomers

William Herschel was a British musician who wanted to become an astronomer so desperately that he built his own 40-foot telescope in his backyard in Bath, with the help of his sister Caroline. The size of a telescope's mirror was directly related to how far an astronomer could see, so the two of them spent over a year creating the largest mirror in the world, ground and polished by hand. Their work paid off: in 1781, William was the first person to discover the planet Uranus, and their mirror was the largest in the world for over fifty years.

**Sister Act**

# Diamonds Are a Girl's Best Friend

During the Middle Ages, there were almost no diamonds in Europe, and the few in circulation were all mined in India. The tradition of diamond engagement rings was born in 1477 when the Austrian archduke Maximillian gave a ring with the letter *M* formed from tiny diamonds to his future bride, Mary of Burgundy. A Parisian spiritualist, Baron d'Orchamps, claimed that wearing a diamond on the third finger of the left hand would both ward off evil and attract good luck, leading to the concept of the "ring finger." And in the mid-eighteenth century, France's Louis XV asked a jeweler to cut a ring reminiscent of the shape of the mouth of his lover, Madame de Pompadour—and the marquise cut was born.

**Memorable Women**

# Chimney Hijinks

Despite Billy the Kid's ferocious reputation, the first act that put him on the wrong side of the law was just a misdemeanor: he helped rob a Chinese laundry, not of cash but clothes. Apprehended almost immediately, he broke out of jail via a chimney—and was on the run until the day of his death.

**Chinese Laundry**
**Wild, Wild West**

## Wild, Wild West
## Kidding Around

One of the most famous outlaws in history was actually a New Yorker: Billy the Kid was born Henry McCarty, probably in New York City's Irish slums, in 1859. He and his mother left the city for New Mexico in the 1870s, but she died in 1874—when her son was only fourteen years old.

**Luck of the Irish**

Billy the Kid became fluent in Spanish when he moved to New Mexico as a boy. The people who gave him refuge in his last days were Spanish-speaking, and his last words were *"¿Quién es?"* which means, "Who's that?"

**Bilingual Education**

McCarty started using the alias William H. Bonney at around age seventeen—the same year he killed a man for the first time, during a barfight in Arizona.

**Famous Barfights**

Billy the Kid was hired by rancher John Tunstall, who was being threatened by a pair of Irishmen who held a monopoly on commerce in Lincoln County, New Mexico. Unnerved by Tunstall's success, the Irishmen sent a posse after him, led by a crooked sheriff. When the posse killed Tunstall, Billy the Kid and several other men swore revenge, which sparked the Lincoln County War: months of conflict between Tunstall's men and the law, culminating in five days of gunfighting in the town of Lincoln. Unable to best the outlaws, the town finally signed a peace agreement with them. Billy the Kid had to flee town once more—but the crooked sheriff had been killed in the "war."

**Bad Cops**

Billy the Kid wasn't a train robber or a bank robber. After the Lincoln County War, where the law was arguably on the wrong side itself, his only crimes against property were rustling. But he reportedly went on to kill nine men before his death at twenty-one, when Sheriff Pat Garrett surprised him in his hideout and shot him.

**Bank Robbers**
**Train Robbers**

## Chinese Laundry

Many early Chinese immigrants to the United States owned or worked in laundries because few other options were open to them due to the Chinese Exclusion Act of 1882, which decreed that Chinese people living in America risked deportation for taking jobs in mining, logging, or manufacturing. But Chinese ownership of laundries was a case of immigrant grit and ingenuity, not training or affinity: China itself didn't have a tradition of commercial laundries at the time.

**European Laundry Techniques**

## Bilingual Education

Fernando Pessoa, one of Portugal's greatest poets, was born in Lisbon but spend his formative years in Durban, South Africa. A great student, but profoundly shy, he rarely spoke with his own classmates, which led to an interesting problem: he learned English from the authors of books from previous centuries, and became fluent in a version of English that no contemporary living English-speakers actually spoke.

**Secrets of Lisbon**

## Sister Act
## Memorable Women

Because of a childhood illness, Caroline Herschel stood only four foot three. Her father educated her over the objections of her mother, and she became a professional musician as well as assistant to her brother William, an amateur astronomer. She may or may not have had a passion for the stars herself—in fact, there's some evidence that she didn't come to stargazing willingly. But when her brother gave her a telescope of her own, she started to discover new comets—eight of them between 1786 and 1797. She was the first woman to discover a new comet, and it was over two hundred years later, with the help of modern technology, before another woman broke her record for most comets found. King George III made William his personal astronomer, with a much smaller pension for Caroline as his assistant, but she may have done the bulk of their work: she did all the math and mapping that supported their discoveries, and when she turned her work in to the Royal Astronomical Society and the Royal Irish Academy after her brother's death, she became the first woman ever to earn honorary membership in either organization.

## Luck of the Irish

## Luck of the Irish

*Luck of the Irish* didn't start out as a compliment. During the California gold rush, many of the best miners were Irish, so jealous competitors started to talk about "the luck of the Irish"—to get across the sly message that Irish people were only successful because of luck, not brains or hard work.

**St. Patrick's Day**

## St. Patrick's Day

During the 1900s, pubs all over Ireland actually *closed* on St. Patrick's Day, because it was a religious observance. The tradition changed in 1970, when the day was recognized as a national holiday and pub doors swung open.

**The Real St. Patrick**

## The Real St. Patrick

St. Patrick is known for wearing green and driving all the snakes from Ireland. But he probably didn't do either. Ireland never had any native snakes and his own preferred color was a pale shade of blue. Green began to dominate his feast day in the late 1700s—around 1,300 years after his lifetime—during the movement for Irish independence.

**No More Snakes**

## No More Snakes

Really hate snakes? Ireland isn't the only place you'd be safe: New Zealand, Iceland, and Greenland are all snake-free. And so is Antarctica, which is good news if you don't mind the cool weather.

**Igloo Living**

## Bank Robbers

Westerns have given us the idea that no bank was safe from robbers in the days of the Wild West, but historians claim that there are more robberies every year in modern-day Dayton, Ohio, than there were in the entire Wild West period, from 1859 to 1900.

**Train Robbers**

## Secrets of Lisbon

Lisbon, Portugal, is home to the world's smallest bookshop, Livraria do Simão. It's only big enough to welcome one shopper at a time—but holds four thousand books.

**World's Biggest Library**

## Train Robbers

Train robberies didn't vanish with the Wild West: one of the most lucrative train robberies in history was pulled off in 1963 in England, by fifteen men, including an antiques dealer, a decorator, a race car driver, a hairdresser, a florist, a nightclub bouncer, and an engineer. The eclectic gang robbed £2.6 million from the Glasgow-to-London mail train—the equivalent of over £50 million today—most of which was never found.

**Crooked Florists**

## World's Biggest Library

The Library of Congress is the world's biggest library, with over 162 million items. But the collection isn't all books: it includes more than one Stradivarius violin, locks of hair from Walt Whitman and Thomas Jefferson, and Amelia Earhart's palm print.

**Libraries Without Books**

## Crooked Florists

Tulips don't come from Holland. They're native to Asia, where a Dutch trader first saw them in Constantinople gardens. He sent samples of the bulbs back home, setting off a frenzy for tulips among the Dutch that resulted in the formation of multiple tulip brokerages over the course of the next century. At the height of the craze, in 1637, tulip prices jumped by more than 1,000 percent in one month, and a single bulb sold for 5,200 florins—or ten times as much as a carpenter made all year. Not long after, the tulip market crashed, bankrupting the whole system. The Dutch government had to wade in to sort the mess out, which took years.

**Constantinople Gardens**

## Constantinople Gardens

The great palace of Constantinople was the residence of the Byzantine kings from the time Constantine I built it, in the early fourth century, until almost a millennium later. Set between the Hagia Sophia and the city circus, the original design included multiple churches, baths, a library, a university, terraced gardens studded with fountains, and a sports field, but later emperors added their own touches.

**Gilding the Lily**

## Gilding the Lily

Two hundred years later, Justinian commissioned a gigantic gilded icon of Christ, the biggest in the city, and covered the main hall, where he received visiting dignitaries, with gilt.

**Top That**

## Top That

Not to be outdone, in the early 800s, Emperor Theophilus hired a mathematician to make a throne that, at the press of the button, could lift him up to the ceiling while a mechanized organ blared. The throne was surrounded by life-sized trees, made from silver and gold, and full of mechanical birds covered with gems. On either side of the throne were lions and griffins, both made of gold, and at the touch of a button, the birds would burst into song, while the lions flicked their tails and let out ferocious roars.

**Tough Act to Follow**

## Tough Act to Follow

Not even fifty years after the rule of Theophilus, Emperor Basil I decided to build himself a brand-new palace *inside* the existing palace, with green stone columns and a ceiling made from glass and gold, as well as a new church with gilt domes, gem-crusted walls, and fountains imported from Venice.

**Where Are They Now?**

## Where Are They Now?

Basil I's beautiful church was blown up in AD 1453, when Turkish invaders used it to store gunpowder. But by that time, Byzantine emperors hadn't lived in the Great Palace for almost three hundred years. During his reign in the first century of the second millennium, Alexios I Komnenos left the ancient buildings for a new palace with more than a dozen chapels and hundreds of rooms. Crusaders looted the palace's holy relics, which wound up in churches in Europe. Which element survived best until the present day? The rich designs of the floor mosaics, which show daily life in the sixth century, when they were first created.

**Holy Smokes!**

## Bad Cops

Chicago police officer Joseph Miedzianowski has the dubious distinction of being the city's dirtiest cop on record. Over his twenty-two years on the beat, many of them as a gang crimes officer, he used police informants, and his power as an officer, to scare off other gangs and build his drug ring—earning him a life sentence in 2003, after his crimes came to light.

**Good Cops**

## Igloo Living

There aren't any igloos in Antarctica, because the famous cold-weather shelters are the invention of Inuit people in Greenland and Canada—who only build them on a relatively small strip of land near Labrador. Igloos aren't made of ice, either: builders cut high, tight-packed snowbanks into blocks, using a sword-like snow knife, and can construct a complete igloo in one or two hours.

**So Much Snow**

## European Laundry Techniques

Before modern detergents were invented, many Europeans used urine in place of soap to clean their clothes. Ancient Romans collected urine from public bathrooms, then watered it down, poured it over a tub of dirty laundry, and had some unlucky servant stomp on it to knock the dirt loose. And it wasn't just the ancient Romans: in various forms, the use of urine to clean clothes in Europe persisted until about 150 years ago.

**Things Made with Urine**

## So Much Snow

Which U.S. state holds the record for the most snowfall in twenty-four hours? You might not be surprised to hear it's Colorado, with a whopping 75+ inches. More surprising: sunny California comes in second, with 67 inches in a single day.

**Winter Sports**

## Good Cops

During the first few years after Oklahoma was opened to settlement, the federal Justice Department spent a fifth of its entire budget policing that single state, which had filled with scoundrels and outlaws during the rush for land. Much of that difficult, dangerous police work was done by Heck Thomas, Bill Tilghman, and Chris Madsen. Known as the "Three Guardsmen," they captured over three hundred outlaws in the newly formed state over the next ten years—and Tilghman lived long enough to star in a movie about his own exploits.

**Police Work**

## Things Made with Urine

In historical formulations, urine was a key ingredient in fabric dye, stain remover, dental care—and gunpowder.

**Good Hygiene**

## Good Hygiene

After the fall of the Roman Empire, bathing got a bad name in Europe. The idea spread that bathhouses, which had been central fixtures in Roman culture, led to all kinds of bad behavior, so public bathing was seen as a sign of bad character—for almost a thousand years.

**What's That Smell?**

## Police Work

It may seem like the friendly neighborhood police officer has always been part of U.S. life, but in fact colonial America only had privately paid officers who worked part-time and focused on whatever a given community was most concerned with: from discouraging prostitution to protecting shipping cargo. But with urbanization, all that changed. Boston was the first city to create a police force paid from public funds, in 1838—largely at the behest of shipping magnates who were tired of paying for protection for their property themselves. But it wasn't until the 1880s that most American cities had a professional police force.

**Shipping Magnates**

## Famous Barfights

The boxer Kid McCoy, welterweight champ, was just trying to have a quiet drink, but when he gave his name to a drunken companion at the same bar, the man insisted that McCoy was lying—he couldn't possibly be the famous pugilist. To prove his point, McCoy laid the belligerent drunk out, and as the disbelieving blowhard got to his feet, he admitted that he'd been vanquished by "the real McCoy."

**Drunken Companions**

## Libraries Without Books

A vault built into a mountainside on an island in the Svalbard archipelago, off the coast of Norway, holds one of the world's most important libraries—but it's full of seeds, not books. The Svalbard Global Seed Vault holds almost a million samples, from African cowpeas to South American potatoes: the most diverse collection in the world—with room to hold almost five times more. In the low temperature of the vaults, the seeds can long outlive the people who placed them there. Lettuce seeds in cold storage are still viable after seventy-three years, while barley can last over two thousand years, and sorghum almost twenty thousand years.

**Old Seeds**

# Old Seeds

The oldest seeds ever known to grow into a plant were those of an Arctic flower called the narrow-leafed campion, planted by researchers in 2007. The seeds were buried 125 feet below Siberian permafrost under the Kolyma River, probably by ancient Arctic ground squirrels that cleverly damaged the seeds to keep them from sprouting in their underground home—but the squirrel colony had at least one or two lazy or clumsy members, because researchers who excavated the ancient squirrel holes found three seeds that were still viable. When modern scientists planted them, the flowers were quite different from modern varieties of the same species, with longer petals, spaced more widely apart. The old seeds proved more fertile, too: 100 percent of the seeds from the plants they produced sprouted, versus only 90 percent of the species' modern seed. And when researchers dated the seeds, they got an even more impressive number: carbon dating showed that the seeds were close to 32,000 years old.

## Dating Methods

## Drunken Companions

While he was Senate majority leader, Lyndon B. Johnson missed very few tricks, and one of his favorites was giving standing orders to his staff to mix his drinks much weaker than those of his companions—so he could keep a clear head as people around him were losing theirs.

**Drunk Presidents**

## Winter Sports

Like skiing and dog sledding, but think they're both a little boring on their own? Try skijoring, where competitors on skis are drawn across a winter landscape by two dogs—or a horse. It was demonstrated at the 1928 Olympics in Switzerland, but for some reason it never caught on.

**Dog Sledding**

## Holy Smokes!
## What's That Smell?

Frankincense, one of the gifts the Wise Men are said to have brought to the infant Jesus, is still one of the most popular incense fragrances in the world, made from the dry sap of trees in the genus *Boswellia*.

**Gifts for Kids**

## Shipping Magnates

Ninety percent of everything we buy travels by ship. But shipowners are a secretive bunch: in Greece, the professional organization of shipowners won't even tell anyone how many members it has.

**Scared of Pirates**

## Dating Methods

In colonial New England, courting was so strictly restricted that a young lady could be charged a fine for kissing in public. To avoid that sad fate, unmarried couples in at least one region communicated through 6-foot-long "courting sticks": tubes that carried their amorous whispers to each other, even though they weren't close enough to touch.

**Crime Waves**

## Gifts for Kids

The invention of the wheel only provokes a great technological leap if you've got beasts of burden to pull your carts around for you. So in the Americas, where there were no large domesticated mammals prior to the arrival of Europeans, the only place wheels appeared were on toys for children.

**Beasts of Burden**

## Scared of Pirates

Modern-day pirates are real—and still dangerous. Today, a ship passenger is more likely to get attacked by pirates than be mugged in South Africa, even though South Africa has the highest crime rate anywhere in the world—on land.

**Crime Waves**

## Dog Sledding

Scientists think that people first hitched dogs to sleds about three thousand years ago. The original sled dogs were probably from Mongolia, migrating with their humans into snowier climes, and they were big—about 75 pounds. But it's not just huskies that can pull a sled—during the Alaska gold rush, when demand for dogs went through the roof, legend has it that all the strays in Seattle were rounded up and pressed into service.

**Through the Roof**

## Beasts of Burden

The closest genetic relative of a horse isn't a cow, deer, or even a camel, but a rhinoceros. Hard as it is to believe, the telltale sign is their feet: horses and rhinos both have odd numbers of toes (rhinos three, horses one), as opposed to the two-toed "cloven hoof" of cattle, deer, and camels.

**Telltale Toes**

# Drunk Presidents

President Ulysses S. Grant is known as a hard drinker, but he didn't get there by partying. While he was a general in the Civil War, doctors prescribed him brandy in hopes of fending off his persistent migraines—which left him with a nasty dependence on the stuff.

**So Much Booze**

When he ran for his first public office—district attorney in Buffalo, New York—Grover Cleveland knew he should cut down on his drinking. So he whittled his intake to just one gallon of beer per day.

**So Much Booze**

President Thomas Jefferson had a wine collection of over twenty thousand bottles—and ran up a bill of about $300,000 in modern-day currency for the alcohol he consumed while in the White House.

**So Much Booze**

## Through the Roof

Because there was virtually no lumber on the Great Plains, early American settlers built what were known as sod houses, shelters dug into the sides of hills. One of their more remarkable features: when it rained, snakes seeking dry ground sometimes dropped into the house from the earthen ceilings.

**Lumberjacks**

## So Much Booze

Edmund G. Booz, who in 1840 opened a Philadelphia distillery that produced Old Cabin Whiskey, was also a genius at promotion: he sold his wares in distinctive cabin-shaped glass bottles and gave away free samples at public events. Legend says that Booz's name became so connected with his product that, in the popular mind, they became synonymous and gave rise to *booze* as a slang term for hard liquor. But linguists say that people have been calling liquor booze since the fourteenth century, so Edmund may have just happened to have a fortunate last name.

**Stuff in Glass**

## Stuff in Glass

Researchers at Vesuvius say that the heat from the famous volcano that exploded in AD 79 near the bustling towns of Pompeii and Herculaneum, capturing many inhabitants in the midst of their daily lives, was so extreme that it turned at least one unlucky Herculaneum resident's brains to glass.

**Ancient Brains**

## Crime Waves

At the turn of the nineteenth century, women were starting to move around freely on their own. Not everybody liked it, and some men liked it a little too much, taking the opportunity to get overly friendly. But women soon discovered that their costumes had armed them with the perfect weapon: hatpins, which were sometimes a whole foot long. When provoked, women began to jam hatpins into offenders' hands, arms, or other appendages. The hatpin crime wave may have reached its peak in a riot in which female factory workers rushed police who had just arrested a pair of their fellow workers over supposedly anarchist speeches. The weapon of choice for the factory workers, who numbered around a hundred? Hatpins.

**Impressive Headgear**

## Lumberjacks

When large-scale logging first began in North America at the end of the 1800s, the word *lumberjack* didn't describe a full-time job but high-paying seasonal work that ambitious farmers picked up in the cold winter months, when their fields were dormant. Traditional lumberjacks, who worked with handsaws that were sometimes many times taller than they were, were replaced by loggers at the advent of power tools, but today logging remains America's most dangerous profession.

**Ambitious Famers**

## Ancient Brains

*Homo sapiens*, or humans, were skinnier than Neanderthals, who would have easily crushed a team of humans in a prehistoric football game. So how did *Homo sapiens* wind up taking the evolutionary lead? They ate meat-rich diets that allowed them to grow bigger brains—which scientists believe led humans to develop better tools, and the language to teach each other how to use them.

**Successful Species**

## Telltale Toes

You've heard of palm readers, but modern-day "sole-ists" read feet. According to them, a long second toe marks you as a leader (like some Egyptian and Hawaiian royal lines). But watch out if the top of someone's third toe is crooked—according to foot readers, that shows a tendency toward deceit.

**Royal Hawaiian**

## Impressive Headgear

In the 1700s, any fashionable man in England had to have a wig. Because they were made from actual human hair, the long, lush wigs of the nobles cost about as much as the average worker made in a whole year. That made them a major luxury item, and a great target for highway brigands, because although a gentleman might not be traveling with a giant bag of money, he would definitely be wearing his wig. The bigger the wig, the richer the wearer— hence the term *bigwig*.

**Why Don't Men Wear Wigs?**

## Why Don't Men Wear Wigs?

The British habit of men wearing wigs went out of fashion very quickly when England instituted a hefty tax on them—but the fact that in the wake of the French Revolution anyone who looked too much like nobility might be executed may have helped, too.

**Angry Frenchmen**

## Successful Species

Humans are the only species on the planet to have successfully established themselves all over the globe.

**The Globe**

## Royal Hawaiian

Lili'uokalani was the last queen of Hawaii, deposed in 1893 by American military acting in the interests of Dole pineapple. She was also a songwriter, and among the 160 songs she penned is "Aloha Oe" (Farewell to Thee), a global hit that's been covered by artists as diverse as Tia Carrere and Johnny Cash.

**The Man in Black**

## Ambitious Farmers

Before the arrival of Spanish conquistadores in the Americas, indigenous famers had developed some of the most sophisticated agricultural techniques on the planet. The famous terraces of Machu Picchu are an ingenious system for making the mountain land arable, conserving soil, limiting erosion, and perhaps even serving as a laboratory that allowed Inca farmers to discover how seeds performed under differing conditions. But Spanish explorers never saw it. The Incas kept its existence secret from outsiders until 1911, when a guide led Professor Hiram Bingham into the mountains, making him the first Western scholar to lay eyes on it.

**Hidden City**

## The Man in Black

The Beatles are famous for using backward masking on their recordings, with sounds played backward into the mix. But Johnny Cash was doing it years before, not just to enhance a recording, but to inspire a song. In 1952, when he served in the U.S. Air Force, he somehow got his hands on a tape of Bavarian guitarists. One day, the tape got put though the machine backward, and the backward guitars gave him the idea for the shushing drone that's the signature of his first huge hit, "I Walk the Line."

**Wild Blue Yonder**

## Angry Frenchmen

The Great Fear refers to the moment in French history when rumors spread among the country's peasants that the aristocracy was plotting against them. In the panic that ensued, Parisians seized the Bastille on July 14, 1789, setting off anti-aristocrat violence across the land. But some historians think that the Great Fear may have been triggered by more than just righteous indignation. Stores of food were low that year, so peasants likely had to eat spoiled grain that may have been infected with ergot, a fungus with hallucinogenic qualities—which scholars believe might have played a part in the general hysteria.

**Long Revolutions**

## Wild Blue Yonder

The U.S. Air Force, the youngest branch of the American military, didn't have an official song until 1938, when a magazine publisher offered a prize for the best composition. Seven hundred entries later, nothing suitable had been found, so contest leaders quietly asked major composers, including Irving Berlin and Meredith Willson, who penned *The Music Man*, for their contributions. But when Robert Crawford, a musician who billed himself as the "Flying Baritone," turned in his entry, it won by unanimous vote.

**Rigging Contests**

## Long Revolutions

In our solar system, Neptune is the farthest planet from the sun, so it has a longer year than any of its companion planets, at almost 165 Earth years. But Neptune spins on its axis faster than Earth does, so a day on Neptune only lasts about sixteen Earthling hours.

**The Longest Day**

# The Globe

Shakespeare is known as a playwright, but he also invented a new business model for theaters. His theater company's original plan was to use the brand-new Blackfriars Theatre. But the Blackfriars district's wealthy neighbors stuck their noses up and refused to let the building be used for something as common as playacting, so Shakespeare and his cronies ponied up their own money, chose another neighborhood, and built the Globe—which meant they got a share in all the profits, not just an actor's salary. The original Globe burned less than twenty years after it was built, set on fire by a real cannon that was apparently being used in a performance of *Henry VIII*. And Puritans dismantled its replacement a few decades after that. But a replica stands in London today—still presenting Shakespeare's plays.

**Snooty Neighbors**

## Hidden City

Atlantis isn't the only sunken city in history. The streets of Baia, an ancient Italian resort, can still be seen through glass-bottomed boats in a bay near Naples, and the ancient Egyptian city of Heracleion, which sank into the ocean over a thousand years ago, was recently discovered underwater about 3 miles from the mouth of the Nile by French explorers on the hunt for sunken warships. Much of the city, where Cleopatra was crowned, is still preserved underwater, including a sphinx, a temple, giant statues, sarcophagi, and over sixty ships.

### Unlucky Resort Towns

We still talk about Atlantis because Plato did, describing a rich and powerful city that sank into the ocean in a single day sometime around 9600 BC. Even in Plato's day, listeners didn't know whether he told the tale as legend or history. But if the story is true, it may be referring to Santorini, a Greek city that was obliterated when the island it was built on erupted around 1600 BC, in what many geologists believe was the biggest volcanic explosion in human history.

### Legendary Lands

Songo Mnara was a thriving Swahili trade center on an island off the coast of Tanzania, until it was abandoned due to power shifts in who controlled nearby trade routes. Built in medieval days, it was famous for its beautiful palace and public pools, and its ruins are still a popular tourist destination.

**City Plans**

Off the coast of Micronesia is a city built on more than a hundred artificial islands, called Nan Madol, constructed in the 1200s. Legend has it that the original builders used magic to fly stone to the new island for houses, businesses, and a royal complex. But the man-made land had no source of water, and the city has been abandoned ever since Europeans arrived in the region in the early 1800s.

**Flying Rocks**

For centuries, La Ciudad Bianca was a tantalizing legend: an ancient city lost in the Honduran rain forest. Charles Lindbergh reported flashes of white buildings amid the greenery, and explorer Theodore Morde claimed he collected hundreds of artifacts in the area in 1939. But it wasn't until 2013 that researchers pinpointed the location with aerial maps—and uncovered the ruins of a previously unknown civilization.

**Shady Explorers**

## The Longest Day

What's the longest day in the history of the world? It's probably sometime next summer. Because Earth's rotation is very gradually slowing down, all our days are getting longer, millisecond by millisecond. So on our long summer days—especially the summer solstice, on June 21 or 22 in the Northern Hemisphere—we're experiencing some of the longest days in history.

**Summer Drinks**

## Rigging Contests

Some regattas draw thousands of ships, and some sailing races circle the globe, but the Bermuda Fitted Dinghy Race might be the most fun to watch. Harking back to a time when Bermudians raced each other to reach big ships that had just arrived in the area—to earn the fee for guiding them through the island's famously treacherous waters—the tiny dinghies are rigged for speed, with so much sail relative to their boat that they would sink under the weight if one member of the crew weren't constantly bailing.

**Bermuda Triangle**

## Unlucky Resort Towns

California's Bombay Beach was created by what seemed to be a stroke of great luck: in 1905, the Colorado River flooded a desert known as the Salton Sink, creating California's biggest lake virtually overnight. Resort attractions sprang up around it, claiming that the "miracle in the desert" was an American Riviera, and by the 1960s, the area boasted not just hotels but a permanent residential community complete with schools. But the desert had no rainfall, and the lake had no outlet, so by the 1970s, the Salton Sea, as it was known, was saltier than the Pacific, and laced with pesticides. As fish died in the increasingly unlivable water, they began to wash up on shore in huge numbers, and today the resort is a ghost town.

**Dead Fish**

## Bermuda Triangle

So many boats and aircraft have disappeared into the Bermuda Triangle—which stretches between Miami, San Juan, and Bermuda—that it's gained a reputation as one of the great mystery spots on the globe, with theorists suggesting everything from transdimensional vortexes to alien abduction to explain the disappearances. But the explanations scientists put forth for the area's uncanny vanishing acts are almost as weird: they include shifts in Earth's magnetic field, and a phenomenon known as "ocean flatulence," in which methane gas bursts out from undersea beds.

**Magnetic Fields**

## Legendary Lands

Peasants in medieval Europe didn't dream of finding El Dorado—they dreamed of Cockaigne, where somehow (even though the sky rained cheese) the rivers were full of wine, the roofs were built from bacon, and you could get paid to sleep.

**Sweet Dreams**

## City Plans

In Manhattan in 1958, at a birthday celebration for Faisal II of Iraq, the architect Frank Lloyd Wright unveiled his master plan for the city of Baghdad. King Faisal approved the design, but that same year he was assassinated by a military cabal, so Wright's design, which featured urban waterfalls and statues of great Islamic kings, never became more than a model.

**Unlikely Waterfalls**

## Flying Rocks

All kinds of space rocks hit our atmosphere each year, but scientists estimate that barely 6,000 of them make it to Earth's surface—and human beings only find about *1 out of 770* of those. Most meteors are smaller than a car and burn up before they hit the ground. But about every two thousand years, a meteor the size of a football field hits Earth. Not to worry, though—in all of recorded history, only one meteorite has ever been known to cause a fatality: a Venezuelan cow expired after being struck by a meteor in 1972.

**Death by Cow**

## Shady Explorers

In 1584, Sir Walter Raleigh got permission to found the first English colony in the Americas, Roanoke. But to get funding for his ventures in the New World, he told a number of tall tales, including claiming to have visited the golden city of El Dorado and having met a race of headless people with eyes in their shoulders, mouths in their chest, and long hair cascading from their backs.

**Tobacco Growers**

## Dead Fish

In 2018, dead fish began to rain on the residents of Fulshear, Texas—as many as a hundred in a single yard. And it wasn't an isolated occurrence—scientists say that dead fish, as well as frogs, spiders, and snakes, are reported falling from the sky, across the globe, about forty times a year. Nobody's sure why, but they're likely caught up in tornadoes—and when they fall, they're often glazed with ice from their time in the upper atmosphere.

**Big Drops**

## Summer Drinks

When the textile heir Barbe-Nicole Ponsardin married the son of her family's competition in the textile business in 1798, the two of them decided to leave the world of textiles behind and invest in a new venture: making wine. But when her husband, François Clicquot, died just a few years after their marriage, Barbe-Nicole found herself in charge of their failing wine business, at the age of just twenty-seven. But Napoleon's defeat in Russia saved her business: she knew the Russians loved champagne, which they'd been missing while at war with France, so she smuggled out almost eleven thousand bottles of her brand in order for it to be the first to hit the Russian market. The czar loved it, and soon she couldn't keep up with demand, so she invented a new way of bottling champagne, still used to this day. But Barbe-Nicole was not the only widow to wind up in charge of a champagne company: Louise Pommery, Lily Bollinger, and Apolline Henriot all took over the helms of champagne makers after their husband's deaths—and grew their businesses into international concerns.

## War Rations

# Magnetic Fields

Earth's magnetic field comes from forces deep inside the planet's molten core that create electric currents that power an invisible magnetic shield. •••••••••

**Journey to the Center of the Earth**

Without this magnetic shield, solar winds would strip Earth's atmosphere of ozone—which makes life on the planet possible.•••

**Animal Magnetism**

Geologic evidence shows that Earth's magnetic field has flipped over time—shown by the way that magnetic elements collect in rocks. ••••

**Animal Magnetism**

The magnetic field around our planet usually weakens about 5 percent per century, but in modern times, it's weakening about 5 percent per decade.•••••••••••••••••••••

**Animal Magnetism**

The British explorer James Ross located magnetic north in the Arctic for the first time in 1831, after his ship had been icebound for four years. No other explorer located magnetic north until the next century. But by the time the Norwegian explorer Roald Amundsen went looking for it, in 1904, it had moved almost thirty miles.

**Arctic Exploration**

In 2019, Earth's magnetic north moved so fast that geomagnetic experts had to create a brand-new World Magnetic Model—which underlies all human navigation, from airplanes to cell phone GPS—a year early.

**Early Cell Phones**

## Unlikely Waterfalls

The deepest and tallest underground waterfall in the United States is Ruby Falls, just outside Chattanooga, Tennessee. It drops a stunning 145 feet in Lookout Mountain Caverns, which is one of the longest in the country.

**Big Drops**

## Snooty Neighbors

The phrase *keeping up with the Joneses* originally came from the title of a comic strip drawn by Arthur R. "Pop" Momand from 1913 to the 1940s. It followed the adventures of the socially striving McGinis family—but the Joneses of the title were never seen once.

**Those Hicks**

## Death by Cow

In the United States, about twenty-two people a year are killed by cattle—while bears kill only three per year.

**Cuddly Bears**

## Sweet Dreams

Despite the popular saying *Sweet dreams*, eating sugar is linked to having nightmares. So are spicy food and alcohol. Even though booze might help you pass out, it leads to bad dreams.

**Surprising Spices**

## Journey to the Center of the Earth

The world's deepest hole is in Kola, Russia, and drops 7.5 miles from Earth's surface. It took twenty years to dig that deep—but the hole isn't even quite halfway through Earth's crust. Drillers gave up when the underground temperatures reached 356 degrees Fahrenheit, almost twice as hot as they expected it to be at that depth. But that's nothing compared to the temperature at Earth's molten core, which is estimated to be around 10,800 degrees Fahrenheit.

**Extreme Air-Conditioning**

## Animal Magnetism

Arctic explorers may have trouble finding true north, but dogs don't: they poop on a north–south axis, in line with Earth's magnetic field.

**Spooky Animals**

## Big Drops

Hail forms when water in the atmosphere is swept up into currents of cold air, creating literal drops of ice. In the United States, the biggest hail falls in South Dakota, where hailstones 8 inches in diameter have been found. The biggest in the world falls in India, where the world's heaviest hailstone—over 2 pounds—touched down. But the world's biggest accumulation of hail may have been in New Mexico, where rain swept hail into a riverbed, piling the chunks of ice into new cliffs along the river that reached 15 feet high.

**Hail Mary**

## Those Hicks

Charles Hicks may have been the last traditional chief of the Cherokee Nation: an avid reader who amassed one of the biggest private libraries anywhere in the United States, he served as the tribe's de facto leader in the years before the Trail of Tears but died after a fall from his horse only two weeks after becoming principal chief. His younger brother stepped in as chief, but almost immediately the tribe dissolved its traditional leadership structure, and the former Indian agent John Ross became leader of the new constitutional republic.

**Big Readers**

## Spooky Animals

You might have heard that dogs can hear things far above the range of human hearing, but elephants' giant ears let them hear sounds far below it—and they can mutter to each other on this subsonic level from as far as 20 miles away.

**Early Cell Phones**

## Early Cell Phones

The first cell phone call was made in 1973, by Martin Cooper of Motorola. He used a prototype of the world's first commercial cell phone, the Motorola DynaTAC 8000x, to call back to his headquarters. The event wasn't recorded for posterity, but Cooper has a vague memory of asking the person who answered about the quality of the sound from their end—which sounds suspiciously like the "Can you hear me? Can you hear me now?" conversation that so many cell phone users still reprise today.

**World's First Text Message**

## Arctic Exploration
## Extreme Air-Conditioning

How do you keep from freezing to death? For Arctic explorers of years past, the answer was often "Sing!" Some expedition leaders actually picked team members for their skills as singers, and an entire genre of songs grew out of the exploration efforts: mostly set to already popular melodies and focused on keeping spirits up across the miles of ice.

**Miles of Ice**

## Tobacco Growers

Cigarettes are the world's most-traded product: a trillion of them are sold across international borders each year. And the world's biggest producer of tobacco is China—although the plant isn't native to Asia.

**Farm to Table**

## World's First Text Message

The world's first text message *might* have been a drunk text: it was sent during a holiday party for Vodafone, a British telecom company, from a twenty-two-year-old engineer named Neil Papworth, to a company executive. The actual text? "Merry Christmas."

**Holiday Parties**

## Cuddly Bears

Did you think pandas couldn't get any cuter? Maybe that's because you've never seen a *tiny baby* panda: they start out pink and black, and only grow in their signature white-and-black markings at about three weeks old.

**Telltale Paw Prints**

## Surprising Spices

Premium saffron costs more per ounce than gold—sometimes twice as much. That's because it comes from the bright red stigmas at the center of the saffron crocus (*Crocus sativus*), and each crocus only has three to five stigmas—which means it takes a hundred blossoms, and a ton of work, to get a gram of saffron.

**Farm to Table**

## War Rations

Food wasn't the only thing rationed in America during World War II—shoes were, too, and in surprising detail. Leather and rubber were both crucial wartime materials, so laws were passed against fancy tongues and trims, heels that were too high, and any colors besides "Army russet," black, brown, and white. As a result, a black market in shoe coupons arose—and manufacturers also got creative about new materials, including carpet, felt, and repurposed firehoses.

**Invisible Enemies**
**First Firemen**

## Hail Mary

The Hail Mary prayer is one of the central prayers associated with the Catholic prayer beads known as the rosary. But early versions of the rosary probably predate the prayer to Mary. The first rosaries may actually have been knotted strings that helped desert monks keep track of their prayers, while reciting all 150 biblical psalms every day.

**Old Songs**

## Invisible Enemies

During World War II, the Allies' Ghost Army, composed largely of artists from New York art schools, created a series of diversions using everything from prerecorded sounds of troop movements to inflatable tanks, to convince the enemy that there were tens of thousands of soldiers in locations where there were only a few hundred. Their most important feat: fooling the Germans into thinking that the bulk of the Allied Forces were miles away from their actual location in the days leading up to the final crossing into Germany at the end of the war—a deception that likely saved thousands of lives, because the Germans, acting on the bad intel, placed their defensive troops in the wrong place.

**Lots of Ghosts**

## Miles of Ice

Ice roads are temporary roads that run over rivers, lakes, or oceans when they freeze, some carefully engineered to last for years. They're a major part of the transport network on the Russian-Chinese border, and an ice road over Lake Ladoga provided the only route to Leningrad when it was under siege in World War II.

**Water Roads**

## Holiday Parties

During the Feast of the Ass, French people in the Middle Ages celebrated the donkey that carried the baby Jesus into Egypt by covering a donkey with jewels and parading it through town to the church. As part of the mock service, the priest would bray at the congregation and the congregation would bray back—after singing a hymn to "Sir Ass."

**Famous Asses**

## Old Songs

Thomas Edison invented the phonograph in 1877, but the first recording of a human voice was made in France in 1860—on *paper*. Édouard-Léon Scott de Martinville created a mechanical device and made several recordings, including one of someone singing a French folk tune, "Au clair de la lune," but he never figured out how to play his recordings, so they were never heard—until 2008, when scientists at a lab in California used a new digital technology to play the folk tune.

**Halfway Solutions**

## Water Roads

The Passage du Gois is a natural spit of land, created by silt buildup and big enough to serve as a road to the French island of Noirmoutier—when it's not underwater. Twice a day, at high tide, the road disappears under waves up to 13 feet deep—sometimes swallowing whole cars.

**High Tide**

## Lots of Ghosts

A house can be called haunted if it's got only one ghost, but in New Orleans two large trees called the Duelling Oaks, in a garden behind the city cathedral, are said to host hundreds of them—from all the fatal duels fought there by touchy eighteenth-century gentlemen.

**If Trees Could Talk**

## Telltale Paw Prints

How do you tell cat tracks from dog tracks? Or perhaps more important, how do you tell if you're following the trail of a bobcat or a coyote? Both dogs and cats leave a four-toed print over a footpad. But dog tracks are much more likely to show claw marks. Cat footpads have three distinct lobes at the bottom, but dogs don't. And the middle two toes of a dog's paw are much closer together than the same two toes of a cat's paw.

**Lonesome Coyotes**

## Farm to Table

Pizza sauce and Bolognese weren't staples of Italian cooking until after Europeans first made contact with Native Americans—the tomato is indigenous to the Andes. • • • • • • • • • • •

**Famous Mountains**

The catastrophic loss of potato crops in Ireland in 1845–49, which led to a huge migration of Irish into the Americas, has fused the potato with Ireland in the popular mind. But the potato is native to Peru and Bolivia. When it was first introduced to Europe, national leaders saw the advantages it offered as a staple crop—unlike wheat, potatoes could lie underground, safer from weather, predators, theft, and pests. And some proponents even observed that, in their opinion, girls who ate primarily potatoes tended to be better-looking. • • • • •

**Beauty Regimens**

Maple syrup is an invention of the Ojibwe people, who gathered in sugar camps to tap trees for their sweet sap as soon as the spring thaw began. • • • • • • • • •

**If Trees Could Talk**

Sweet Potatoes are a staple in several African cuisines, but they're native to the Americas, first brought to Africa by the Portuguese.

**Orange Food**

## Orange Food

Carrots appear in dishes worldwide, from American pot roast to Chinese fried rice, but they were originally cultivated in Persia.

**Hungry Bunnies**

If you listen to fruit juice companies, you might think oranges originated in Florida—but they're native to China, along with apricots.

**Forbidden Fruit**

## Hungry Bunnies

In 1859, an English colonist in Australia, Thomas Austin, released two dozen rabbits on his property to provide some sport for local hunters—not realizing that they had almost no natural predators on the continent. Not even forty years later, the progeny of those first bunnies had done so much agricultural damage that the country spent six years erecting the largest unbroken fence in the world—over 1,100 miles. And in the century since then, no better solution has been found to fend off the toothsome critters, so the fence still stands.

**Natural Predators**

## Lonesome Coyotes

Coyotes often hunt alone, unlike wolves, which often hunt in packs. Perhaps because of this, coyotes can survive in small territories—which may be why so many have migrated to urban centers, including one coyote family that raised an entire litter of puppies in the parking lot at Chicago's Soldier Field. Today, there are coyote populations in almost every U.S. city.

**Wolf Packs**

## First Firemen

The first Roman fire brigade was a for-profit effort. Marcus Licinius Crassus organized five hundred men trained to rush to the site of burning buildings—but they wouldn't lift a finger until the building's owner offered to pay.

**Expensive Water**

## Famous Asses

Winnie-the-Pooh's friend the stuffed donkey Eeyore is famous for his mopey pronouncements. But his depressive moods may have been drawn from life, since Pooh author A. A. Milne suffered from PTSD after his experiences in World War I.

**Talking Animals**

## High Tide

Canada's Bay of Fundy experiences the highest tides in the world: 53 feet above low tide, the water rolls in over 174 miles of shoreline, twice a day.

**Awesome Canadians**

## Big Readers

In the early 1500s, the Spaniard Hernando Colón, son of Christopher Columbus, decided he wanted to create a library that contained everything: not just published books but all written matter, from unpublished manuscripts to tavern posters. Colón, who also collected music and plants, created a library of over fifteen thousand books—so many he was forced to invent the bookshelf as we know it today, where books stand side by side, spine to spine. But Colón's quest to collect all the knowledge of the known world had a tragic element: at the beginning of his life, it might have been possible to collect all the knowledge of the known world, but because he lived at a time of vast advances in printing technology, the creation of new books far outstripped his ability to collect them.

## Unpublished Manuscripts

## Expensive Water

Denmark's got the most expensive tap water in the world: at Danish rates, the average American would pay over $3,000 a year in water bills. But that may just be because the Danes are doing good accounting to make sure the price of their water really covers all their costs. Turns out, many water services around the globe don't actually charge as much as it costs to get the water to their customers, so a lot of us are drinking subsidized water.

**Bad Accounting**

## Halfway Solutions

Test pilot Joe Cotton was thrilled to fly the 1966 Valkyrie XB-70, the finest plane of its day—until the front landing gear jammed. Convinced that the plane would crash with the nose gear at the wrong setting, Cotton used a paper clip to bypass the plane's circuit breaker, saving the plane, which would be worth $5.5 billion in today's dollars.

**Norse Myths**

## If Trees Could Talk
## Talking Animals
## Forbidden Fruit

The Bible doesn't specifically name the fruit the snake conned Adam and Eve into eating in the Garden of Eden, so why do we tend to think it's an apple today? Some historians think it's a kind of ancient pun: the Latin word for "apple," *malum*, is spelled the same as the word for "evil"—which may have given rise to the idea of apple as forbidden fruit.

**Important Apples**

## Awesome Canadians
## Famous Mountains

Some of the freshest water in the world can be found in the Canadian Rockies, at the Columbia Icefield. It's the hydrographic peak for North America, and water that melts from the icefields flows up to the Arctic Ocean, and all the way to the Atlantic and the Pacific, on opposite sides of the continent.

**Fresh Water**

## Unpublished Manuscripts

Ernest Hemingway's first novel was never published, because it was stolen. His wife, Hadley, was bringing a bag full of all his early manuscripts to him, from Paris to Lausanne, but someone stole it from her seat when she got off the train to buy a bottle of Evian water.

**Fresh Water**

## Beauty Regimens

Ancient Egyptian lipsticks were dyed with iodine and a plant-based chemical, bromine mannite, that gave them a deep purple hue but also caused seizures and psychotic episodes, and sometimes killed wearers—or people who had shared a kiss with them—which may be where we got the phrase *the kiss of death*. The original lipstick chemistry was so toxic that extracting dye from beetles and ants seemed like a better bet—the ingredients of the famous red carmine pigment.

**Candy Apple Red**

## Natural Predators

The African lion today roams free only in sub-Saharan Africa and India. But archaeological evidence shows that the lion was once the apex predator throughout Africa and the Middle East, from India to the Mediterranean.

## Roaming Mammals

Polar bears are the apex predator of the of the Arctic Circle, and the biggest on land, topping out at 1,500 pounds.

## The Antarctic Circle

The Komodo dragon is the apex predator of the smallest territory: a single island in the Pacific. But it's also the largest lizard anywhere on earth. And its bulk doesn't make it slow: Komodo dragons can run up to 20 miles per hour.

## Breathing Fire

Saltwater crocodiles are northern Australia's apex predators, and the most dangerous to humans, killing about a thousand people per year globally. They're 20 feet long, weigh over 2,000 pounds, and eat almost anything, which may explain the Australian government's official policy toward crocs: avoid them at all costs.

**Crocodile Tears**

Orcas, also known as killer whales, are the top apex predator worldwide, because they're the top apex predator in all oceans. It's not because they're the biggest. Orcas have been known to hunt creatures five times larger than they are. But they're highly intelligent, communicate well in teams, and hunt just about anything in the sea.

**Sea World**

## Bad Accounting

Enron, the company at the center of the biggest fraud case in U.S. history, started out selling natural gas but wound up selling derivatives for electricity, steel, paper—and weather. But as the boom of the 1990s faded, the company began to engage in some shady accounting, known as "mark-to-market," which allowed executives to write future gains into current income statements, basically inventing profits. When outside analysts got a look at Enron's financial statements in 2001, the company's stock market value was wiped out, along with the retirement accounts of thousands of employees—and Enron's accounting firm, Arthur Andersen, which had been among the most prestigious in the world, surrendered its license to practice.

## Weather Reports

## Norse Myths
## Important Apples

In Norse mythology, Idun is the goddess of spring, youth, and renewal, but her most important job is keeping the gods themselves alive. Norse gods aren't immortal, so they have to eat Idun's magic apples to stay young.

**Eat Your Fruit**

## Roaming Mammals
## Wolf Packs

Wolves used to have the widest distribution of any mammal on the planet—except humans. But the expansion of human habitats has reduced the range of wolves by a third.

**Greedy Creatures**

## Sea World

Over three-quarters of Earth is covered with water—but 80 percent of the world's oceans have not been mapped—or even observed.

**Fresh Water**

## Weather Reports

American weather prediction is a relatively new science, barely a hundred years old. But residents of the Caribbean developed ways to read the weather much earlier, because tropical storms meant the weather was often a matter of life or death. But when American settlers first migrated to regions where tropical storms played a big role in the weather, they ignored the warnings of their neighbors to the south—which led to enormous loss of life during the hurricane that literally wiped most of Galveston, Texas, from the map in 1900. It remains the largest loss of life due to a natural disaster in the history of the United States.

**Bigger in Texas**

## Crocodile Tears

Crocodiles really do cry, but not because they're sad. They're liable to gulp too much air when eating, which puts pressure on their tear glands, squeezing out tears.

**Big Crybabies**

## Eat Your Fruit
## Candy Apple Red

Candy apples were invented in New Jersey in 1908, by William Kolb, a Newark candymaker who used the red cinnamon coating to create a bright window display. He thought the shiny apples would lure people in to buy his regular stock of candies—but it turned out customers wanted the apples, which were soon sold at the Jersey Shore, then around the globe.

**Jersey Shore**

## Bigger in Texas

Texas is the only state in the Union that is allowed to divide itself into other states. West Virginia, for example, can't legally decide to become West Virginia and East West Virginia, but Texas can legally subdivide into up to five new American states, according to the agreement it made when entering the Union.

**Altered States**

## Breathing Fire

Dragons might be a myth, but they're a persistent and widespread one: scientists think that belief in dragons emerged independently in China, Europe, the Americas, and even Australia. But wherever the myths emerged, dragons all had key details in common: they're greedy, they're grouchy, and they all breathe fire.

### Greedy Creatures

## Jersey Shore

The shark that stalked the coast of New Jersey in the summer of 1916 didn't just prowl the beaches—it actually swam miles upstream into Matawan Creek, to attack a group of boys at a favorite swimming hole. The panic inspired by multiple attacks that summer may have been part of the inspiration for the blockbuster *Jaws*—but the real-life story has a twist: when scientists got their hands on the shark believed to be the culprit, it turned out to be a bull shark, not a great white.

### The Female of the Species

## Big Crybabies

Humans are the only animals that shed tears when we're sad.

**Get Happy**

## Altered States

Michigan almost entered the United States without the Upper Peninsula: as its borders were being established, one option on the table was giving those northern regions to Ohio—in exchange for Toledo.

**Bad Trades**

## Greedy Creatures

Scientists estimate that hummingbirds have to eat two to three times their own body weight per day—more than any other animal that's not an insect, and the equivalent of a human eating thirty hamburgers daily. But it's brain food— their brains are twice as large as human brains, relative to their body weight.

**Vital Organs**

## The Antarctic Circle

The Arctic Circle, to the north of the globe, got a lot of attention from European explorers—because it was a whole hemisphere closer than the Antarctic, at the south. But the Arctic is really only a vast ocean, covered with ice, while Antarctica is an actual continent.

**Down Under**

In Antarctica's Dry Valleys, the driest land on earth, low temperatures mean there's so little humidity that snow and ice can't build up.

**Just Desserts**

The highest mountains in the world—the Gamburtsev—are in Antarctica, although they're mostly stuck in ice.

**Roadside Assistance**

Antarctica has an active volcano *under the ice*, on Deception Island. The ice above it is so thick that even when it erupts with molten lava, it still doesn't break through to the surface.

**Lava Lamps**

In 2010, explorers discovered an Antarctic trench 62 miles long and almost twice as deep as the Grand Canyon—still with no name.

**Down Under**

In recorded history, only ten humans have been born in Antarctica—the first in 1979.

**High Birthrates**

## Get Happy

The Partridge Family was a fictitious act, but they got a very real Grammy nomination for best new group of 1970.

### Family Acts

## Vital Organs

For over a thousand years before the Industrial Revolution, the pipe organ, which was invented two hundred years before the birth of Christ by a Greek engineer, Ctesibius, was the most complex machinery humans had ever created.

### Complex Machines

## Bad Trades

Babe Ruth started his career with the Boston Red Sox, but when owner Harry Frazee decided to dabble as a theatrical producer, his costs began to soar and he traded Ruth to the Yankees in 1919. With Ruth on the team, the Yankees won four World Series victories—while the Red Sox didn't score one for another eighty-six years.

### Expensive Shows

## Just Desserts

Two hundred years ago, Americans ate about 2 pounds of sugar per year. Today, we eat about 152 pounds per year—or 3 pounds per week.

**Losing Pounds**

## High Birthrates Down Under

Grey kangaroo births are pretty painless for kangaroo moms, because when joeys squirm into their famous pouches, they're only about the size of a kernel of corn. Once they find a nipple and latch on inside the pouch, they'll stay there for over a year. But once that joey starts to venture outside the pouch, another tiny joey will be born into it—and the kangaroo mom will start producing two very different kinds of milk. Not only that, but while the littlest one is nursing, mom will also be incubating a third joey, ready to be born as soon as the second one is strong enough to clamber out of the pouch.

**Family Acts**

## Fresh Water

The Great Lakes are the largest system of freshwater in the world, with 20 percent of the freshwater on the globe. Over 50 percent of the rest of the world's freshwater reserves are in Antarctica, stored as ice.

**Great Lakes Ships**

## Roadside Assistance

Roman roads were the key to the empire's military might, because even the best army in the world won't help you much if it can't get anywhere. Roman engineers learned to make durable roadways from whatever was at hand, all over the empire. Less known is the fact that the network was served by state-run roadhouses, about every 10 miles, where travelers could trade in their horses for a fresh one, and state-run hotels every 20 miles. Perhaps most important: Roman roads were patrolled by soldiers who chased away would-be bandits—and also collected tolls.

**World's Greatest Roads**

# Great Lakes Ships

You can't usually sail an ocean liner on a little lake. The Great Lakes, though, are large enough for oceangoing loads. But because they're not *quite* as big as the open ocean, the Great Lakes don't have such big waves. So Great Lakes ships have a profile that's unique on the globe: much longer and lower to the water than any other large boats.

**Great Lakes Shipwrecks**

# Losing Pounds

In 1927, the sports agent C. C. Pyle organized the Transcontinental Footrace, which stretched between Santa Monica and New York City, and was accompanied by a carnival complete with a dog who could communicate by twitching his ears and a mummified outlaw. But barely a quarter of the 199 runners who started were able to finish the race—because the punishing schedule of 3,424 miles in under two months meant that it was humanly impossible for most of them to maintain their body weight.

**Expensive Shows**

## The Female of the Species

Unlike male lions, lionesses stay in the same region all their life, which gives them invaluable knowledge of local resources and threats. But they're not afraid to fight: as hunters, defending their region, and to protect cubs from aggressive older males. • • • •

**No Place Like Home**

On the seas, female orcas lead their pods of apex predators for a similar reason—they stick to the waters where they were born all their lives, and can live into their nineties, so nobody knows the place like they do. • • • • • • •

**No Place Like Home**

Female hyenas are bigger than males, and in any kind of fight, they're the ones on the front lines. • • • • • • • • •

**Battle Lines**

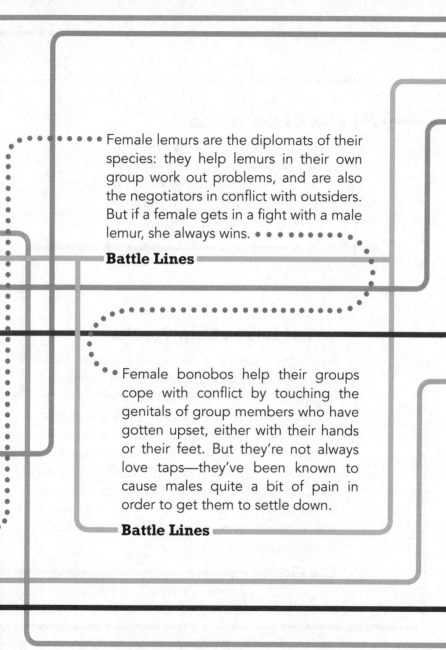

Female lemurs are the diplomats of their species: they help lemurs in their own group work out problems, and are also the negotiators in conflict with outsiders. But if a female gets in a fight with a male lemur, she always wins.

**Battle Lines**

Female bonobos help their groups cope with conflict by touching the genitals of group members who have gotten upset, either with their hands or their feet. But they're not always love taps—they've been known to cause males quite a bit of pain in order to get them to settle down.

**Battle Lines**

## No Place Like Home

*The Wizard of Oz*, starring Judy Garland, was a huge flop when it debuted in 1939. It wasn't until 1956, when it began to be rebroadcast on television, that it became one of America's best-loved films.

**Big Flops**

## Great Lakes Shipwrecks

Ships don't usually sink way out at sea. More often, they break up on land as they're headed for shelter. So the Great Lakes, which have far more shoreline relative to their surface area than the open seas, have huge numbers of shipwrecks. Because of the frigid, clean water, the wrecks are often beautifully preserved, even a hundred years later. But because so many ships broke up in the same places, it can be hard to tell which wreckage—or eerily preserved victims—belong to which ships.

**Old Pickles**

## Battle Lines

"Damn the torpedoes, full speed ahead!" is one of the most famous lines ever spoken in battle. But it was uttered by Union vice admiral David Farragut during an attack on Mobile Bay, Alabama, during the Civil War—even though the below-the-surface, self-guided missile we now know as the torpedo wasn't invented until 1866, by an Englishman name Robert Whitehead, who was working for the Austro-Hungarian government. So what was Farragut talking about? Underwater Confederate mines, which were called torpedoes at the time.

**Takes Guts**

## Old Pickles

The first pickles in the world, which were put up over four thousand years ago, were a lot like the ones we eat today: Mesopotamian cucumbers, preserved in brine.

**Weird Cravings**

## Family Acts

Francis Ford Coppola, director of *The Godfather*, along with dozens of other films, is one of the biggest names in Hollywood history, so it's not a surprise that his kids, Sofia and Roman, have both made names for themselves as filmmakers. Less well-known: he's uncle both to Jason Schwartzman, his sister's son, and Nicolas Cage, his brother's.

## Big Flops

## Weird Cravings

People have been eating dirt since prehistoric times, around the world, and some still crave it today, especially pregnant women. Dirt doesn't have any nutritional value, so the cravings have long been a mystery, but scientists now suspect that certain types of dirt—in particular, a chalky white clay called kaolin—may leach toxins from the gut.

## Takes Guts

## Takes Guts

Catgut is a durable cord used to string violins, tennis rackets, and bows for archery, as well as in surgical applications. It's made from animal intestines but not usually from cats—more commonly it comes from sheep.

**Bows and Arrows**

## Expensive Shows
## Big Flops

The director Francis Ford Coppola spent so much money on *Apocalypse Now* that to make amends, he agreed to make *One from the Heart*, a musical about a couple whose marriage is on the rocks, set in Las Vegas on the Fourth of July. It was budgeted at a modest $13 million, but Coppola came in over budget again at more than $23 million—and it brought in only $1 million at the box office.

**Real Howlers**

## World's Greatest Roads

The Silk Road was the longest network of trade routes in the ancient world, stretching 4,000 miles, from the Chinese city of Xi'an to Constantinople, by way of India and Persia.

### Road Trips

The Silk Road's complete routes were first established around 130 BC when the Han dynasty opened to trade with the West. Vibrant trade along the routes lasted for well over a thousand years, until the Ottoman Empire refused further trade with the West, in 1453.

### Famous Boycotts

The Silk Road was largely founded on the Persian Royal Road, built in 500 BC, which ran from Susa to the Mediterranean Sea. Postal stations along the Persian Royal Road kept fresh horses for messengers, who moved so fast and efficiently that Herodotus wrote, "Neither snow, nor rain, nor heat, nor darkness of night prevents these couriers from completing their designated stages with utmost speed"—now the motto of the U.S. Postal Service.

### Postal Service

What was worth traveling 4,000 miles for? People in the East were eager for Western goods like horses, dogs, furs, grapes, honey, glassware, and weaponry, while people in the West couldn't get enough of eastern silk, dyes, gems, porcelain, medicine, perfume, rice, paper, spices, and gunpowder. But perhaps the most important import, on all sides, was culture: it was the Silk Road that brought Buddhism to China and the bubonic plague to the Byzantine empire—and the great exchange of ideas along the route laid the foundation for the rise and fall of multiple empires, and the Renaissance in Europe.

**Boom!**

When the Silk Road closed, European explorers, desperate for goods from the East, took to the sea to find alternate routes—and eventually "discovered" the Americas.

**Alternate Routes**

## Real Howlers

Wolves and coyotes aren't the only creatures that howl at the moon. The grasshopper mouse, which hunts scorpions in the deserts of the American southwest, earned the name "werewolf mouse" because it emits a tiny nocturnal wailing to mark its territory.

**Werewolves of London**

## Bows and Arrows

Medieval European archers used fiery arrows to great effect, because medieval Europe was mostly built out of wood. Fire arrowheads were specially formed to stick better in thatched roofs, then coated in resin or oil, or wrapped in cotton and set alight. But contemporary Muslim troops were even better equipped, with arrows fitted with glass vials full of an explosive that detonated into flames on contact.

**Fire Works**

## Lava Lamps

Edward Craven Walker, an English accountant, got a bright idea for a new kind of lamp in 1948 from watching the liquids bubble in a cocktail shaker someone left on a pub's stove. Fifteen years of experimentation later, he unveiled the lava lamp, which went on to sell at a rate of seven million per year in its 1970s heyday.

**Complex Machines**

## Boom!

Gunpowder was invented in China in AD 808, but its first application was as a medicine. It wasn't used for military purposes for almost another hundred years.

**Fire Works**

## Complex Machines

The six space shuttles built by NASA starting in the 1970s were the most complicated machines in the history of humankind, each with over 2.5 million parts. Over a thousand of those were plumbing valves. Each shuttle also contained more than 200 miles of wire, all protected by 27,000 insulating tiles.

**Too Much Wire**
**Lost in Space**

## Road Trips
## Alternate Routes

Bill Doolin, the most successful train robber in American history, was killed by a posse in Lawson, Oklahoma, as he tried to sneak away from his wife's house under cover of darkness. There were four other roads he could have taken out of town that night—but he made the mistake of choosing the one his wife warned him not to take, which turned out to be the only one that was guarded.

**Desperate Bandits**

# Famous Boycotts

In 1880, British land agent Charles Cunningham Boycott, known for his harsh and sometimes bloody eviction of Irish tenants on behalf of landowner Lord Erne, tried to evict eleven more tenants. But the Irish of County Mayo had had enough. They refused to labor on Erne's lands or serve Boycott in local shops, and sent threats to his blacksmith, laundress, and messenger boy. It was Boycott who made his name famous worldwide—by complaining to the English press about the situation. Newspapers from around the globe sent correspondents to the county, where laborers had to be hired from other regions because local laborers refused to work for Boycott. Under the guard of more than a thousand men, Boycott's scabs brought in the harvest at a cost of £10,000—twenty times what the £500 crop was even worth. Disgraced, Boycott left Ireland that winter, never to return.

## Angry Blacksmiths

## Fire Works

The first fireworks were invented around AD 1000 by Li Tan, a Chinese monk who jammed gunpowder into a length of bamboo and tossed the whole thing in a fire. The pop and flash were so delightful that fireworks became an integral part of Chinese New Year celebrations, weddings, and military displays. Italians added colors to the mix by experimenting with new metals during the Renaissance. But it was John Adams who made them an American tradition: on July 3, 1776, he wrote his wife, Abigail, that the celebrations around the Declaration of Independence should include "Illuminations from one End of this Continent to the other . . . forever more." The next day, among the ringing of bells in Philadelphia, crowds were treated to a giant fireworks display that began and ended with the firing of thirteen rockets—and started a national tradition.

## Rowdy Weddings

## Postal Service

The South Pacific island of Vanuatu boasts the world's only underwater post office, where divers can mail waterproof postcards. But it may not be Vanuatu's craziest postal outpost: the island's postal service also has an office just steps away from the crater of an active, magma-spewing volcano.

**Deep Dives** ━━━━━━━━━━━

## Werewolves of London

Despite Warren Zevon's huge 1978 pop hit, "Werewolves of London," the world's biggest werewolf craze probably began with a spate of 1500s trials in Switzerland. Perhaps most famous: an unlucky German named Peter Stump. Neighbors claimed that after a local werewolf had its paw cut off, Stump showed up without one of his hands. During a wild trial, Stump confessed that the devil had given him a magic girdle that turned him into a wolf, but it didn't help his case: he was sentenced to be burned to death, and for the next two centuries, people were tried as werewolves all over Europe.

**Mister and Mistress** ━━━━━━━━━━━

## Too Much Wire

John Roebling, who designed the Brooklyn Bridge, was a manufacturer of wire rope who took bridge-building gigs to drive demand for his product. After stringing suspension bridges all over the Midwest, he drew plans for the Brooklyn Bridge. But he died before it was completed, from tetanus, after his foot was crushed by a ferry while he was choosing a location for the bridge on the East River.

**Who Built the Brooklyn Bridge?**

## Lost in Space

It's no surprise that astronauts have lost gloves, tools, and cameras in space, since they're pretty easy to lose track of on earth. But one of the major things early astronauts left behind in orbit is pee, which freezes almost instantly into tiny floating crystals when its released from a ship. The International Space Station now has a system that recycles urine into drinking water, but several of the first astronauts say that watching pee crystals float into the cosmos is one of the most beautiful things they've ever seen.

**Beauty Standards**

## Desperate Bandits

Robin Hood may have just been a nickname for any kind of English bandit, dating back to the 1300s. There's no evidence a single person with that name really existed, although contemporary writers clearly believe he did. But the stories of the bandit who robbed from the rich to give to the poor are so beloved that sometimes they appear to attach to modern bandits. In a 1450 story, a character named Robyn Hode loans a broke knight £400 to pay off a crooked priest, then robs the priest to get the money back. And tales say that the U.S. outlaw Jesse James gave a widow hundreds of dollars to save her farm from a greedy banker, then robbed the banker to reclaim his cash.

**Outlaw Afterlives**

## Rowdy Weddings

Matching bridesmaids dresses didn't start out as a fashion statement: in Roman days, women wearing identical garb would surround the bride on her way to the groom's home and act as bodyguards if jealous lovers tried to kidnap her or bandits appeared to nab the dowry.

**Mister and Mistress**

## Mister and Mistress

England is the only country in Europe where it was common for women to take their husband's last name after marriage—because by law, at marriage, her husband took all her property. Until around 1800, married women were addressed along with their first name: "Mrs. Felicity Smith." Around 1800, even women's first names were dropped, in favor of the shorter "Mrs. Smith." But not even a generation later, women were already angling to keep more of their own names. In the United States in 2020, around 20 percent of women kept their last name after marriage, with another 10 percent opting for one that was hyphenated or blended.

**Single Ladies**

## Angry Blacksmiths

*Smith* has been the most common name in English for over a hundred years. It probably comes from the word *smite*, "to hit," which makes sense if you recall that a smith is someone who spends his days striking metal.

**Big Hits**

## Outlaw Afterlives

The outlaw Jesse James died in a Missouri shootout in 1882, but his brother, Frank, survived to get a job as a shoe salesman in Dallas.

**Good Shoes**

# Who Built the Brooklyn Bridge?

After John Roebling's death, his oldest son, Washington Roebling, took charge of building the Brooklyn Bridge. But just a few years later, he was struck with the bends after returning to the surface from a watertight chamber sunk below the river and never recovered. He spent the final years of the build watching its progress from his home near the river, through a telescope, while his wife, Emily, transmitted his notes to other engineers and builders, serving as his presence on the site and managing the entire project to completion in his place as chief engineer.

**Engineering Tests**

## Single Ladies

When Beyoncé broke the record for most Grammys won in one year by a single woman, three of them were for "Single Ladies": Song of the Year, Best R&B Song, and Best Female R&B Performance.

**Rhythm and Blues**

## Deep Dives

The fish that dwells deepest in the ocean is the snailfish, which makes its home 5 miles below the surface in the Mariana Trench, well below the 1.5-mile mark, where protein begins to destabilize under the enormous pressure. The snailfish's pink skin is so translucent that you can clearly see its organs, and though it's only a little more than a foot long, its body can withstand water pressure equal to the weight of two thousand pickup trucks.

**Big Trucks**

## Big Hits
## Rhythm and Blues

Motown Records has the highest hit rate of any music company in history. Between 1960 and 1970, the hitmakers at Motown put out 535 singles and 375 of them landed in the Top 40, which means that 70 percent of all the singles Motown released charted, for an entire decade.

**Motor City**

## Engineering Tests

When the Brooklyn Bridge was completed, the general public remained suspicious that the design's signature web of wire could support heavy traffic—so P. T. Barnum marched twenty-one elephants, including his famous Jumbo, across the span to ease their fears.

**Spiderwebs**

## Beauty Standards
## Good Shoes

Men were the first to wear high-heeled shoes, and originally it wasn't a fashion statement, but a practical necessity—they needed something to keep their feet from slipping through their stirrups while on horseback. But since owning a horse cost money, wearing high heels became a way to show off your status—even when you didn't have your horse.

**Horse Power**

## Big Trucks

The biggest trucks in the world aren't on the road. They're used in mining. Weighing in at about a million pounds themselves, they're built to carry 300 tons of ore in a single load.

**Mine Craft**

## Horse Power

James Watt, the Scottish engineer who lent his name to "wattage," was also the first to define the notion of horsepower. He used the concept to compare the work of a horse to the work of the steam engines he was perfecting. But 1 horsepower doesn't always equal the work of one horse. At peak performance, a single horse is capable of exerting almost 15 horsepower.

### Different Fuels

## Spiderwebs

Spiders are some of the smartest animals in the world, with the ability to plan, solve complex problems, and even be surprised. But if you take their web away, they're not as smart, leading researchers to believe they use the web to think.

### Thinking Machines

## Motor City

Henry Ford helped create the U.S. middle class with the five-dollar day—paying workers in his automobile factories almost twice as much as they could make elsewhere. But he had to, in order for his company to survive. The first assembly-line workers hated doing the same task all day long so much that, before the pay hike, Ford had sky-high rates of absenteeism and drinking on the job.

**Drinking on the Job**

## Different Fuels

The first oil well was drilled in Titusville, Pennsylvania, in 1859. Drillers knew that crude oil might have industrial applications, but they had no idea that there were huge deposits in Texas and the Middle East—so for a brief period, Pennsylvania was the capital of the world's oil industry.

**Huge Deposits**

## Huge Deposits

As of 2020, JPMorgan Chase held more deposits than any other bank in the world, with over $1.9 trillion.

**Thrill of the Chase**

## Drinking on the Job

Christian monks drink wine whenever they take the Eucharist, and perhaps as a result, they've been central to major developments in drinking, including the Benedictine monk Dom Pierre Pérignon, a pioneer in the creation of champagne, and Arnold of Soissons, who invented the filtration of beer in the eleventh century—and was made a saint.

**Second Rounds**

## Mine Craft

In the next decades, there may be more mining operations below the ocean than on land—undersea mountains contain the same kinds of deposits as on dry land and have barely been tapped yet. But they'll look very different from the big timbers and cramped corridors of traditional land mining: the primary technique in current ocean mining is dredging up material from the ocean bed, not drilling or digging.

**Big Timbers**

## Second Rounds

Before World War II, no one referred to World War I as World War I, because they didn't realize there was going to be another one. They called it the Great War or, more poignantly, the War to End All Wars—not realizing that another conflict would engulf much of the world less than a generation later.

**Next Generation**

## Thinking Machines

Babylonian mathematician Abu Ja'far Muhammad ibn Musa al-Khwarizmi wrote at Baghdad's House of Wisdom in the early 800s, and introduced a number of new mathematical concepts to his readers in Europe. The Arabic word for "transposition," *al-jabr*, from the title of one of his most famous works, is where English gets the word *algebra*—and also *algorithm*, the basis for all modern computing.

**Big Nerds**

## Thrill of the Chase

Cars burst into glorious flame in almost every Hollywood car chase—but almost never in real life. In the United States each year, only about 8,100 vehicles catch fire after a crash—out of well over 7 million accidents, a vanishingly small fraction.

**Vanishingly Small**

## Big Timbers

The world's tallest tree is a California redwood, discovered in 2006, and topping out at just over 380 feet tall. Nicknamed "Hyperion," its location is a closely guarded secret. Why? Maybe because during the California gold rush, men spent three weeks cutting down the biggest redwood they could find, even though it was 1,244 years old, and then held dances on the stump—which caused so much outrage when it was reported by the press that it helped kick-start the modern conservation movement.

## Minor Titans

## Vanishingly Small

The smallest flower in the world is green and belongs to the watermeal, a species of duckweed that floats on the surface of undisturbed ponds. The tiny blooms are much smaller than a grain of rice: hundreds can fit on the tip of a human finger.

## Crazy Swamps

## Big Nerds

Apple Computer cofounder Steve Jobs might get a lot of credit for his company's famous machines, but Nikola Tesla, who was born in the midst of a lightning storm, not only invented wireless technology but also came up with the idea for a handheld wireless device—in 1901. At his death in 1943, the U.S. government's Office of Alien Property seized everything he owned—and although they gave most of it back to his family, some of Tesla's work is still officially classified, and some of his possessions are still impounded in government lockup.

**Alien Sightings**

At the time the Italian inventor Guglielmo Marconi began experimenting with wireless technology, at the end of the 1800s, the most prominent scientists in the world believed it would never transmit farther than across a room. But Marconi built massive transmitters on his own family property in Italy and had his brother stand by with a flare gun to confirm that his signals did in fact carry across the beautiful Italian hills.

**Mistaken Scientists**

Marie Curie's husband, Pierre, was studying crystals and electricity when they met, but it was Marie who got interested in the strange rays that radiated from salts laced with uranium. Her experiments led her to coin the word *radioactivity*—and her continued work with Pierre laid the foundation of our understanding of it today. Pierre died after being run over by a horse-drawn carriage less than a decade after his wife's discovery, and she took his place as the first female professor at the Sorbonne and continued her work for almost another thirty years, before dying of a blood disease due to exposure to radiation.

**Bad Blood**

Over thirty years, gaming-store operator Michael Thomasson amassed the world's biggest collection of video games, at over 11,000. Of these, 8,300 still had their box and manual, and 2,600 had never had their shrink-wrap broken. The whole collection sold for $750,000 in 2014.

**Favorite Games**

## Next Generation

Of the first five *Star Trek* series captains, the only one who's not an American is Jean-Luc Picard, who hails from La Barre, a town in France. The original Captain Kirk's hometown was Riverside, Iowa. Captain Sisko of *Deep Space Nine* came from New Orleans. Captain Kathryn Janeway, of the *Voyager* series, grew up in Bloomington, Indiana, and Captain Jonathan Archer, of the *Enterprise*, came from New York State.

**Big Easy**

## Minor Titans

One of the earliest myths in Greek history is of the Titans, the twelve children of the earth and sky who ruled the world before their own children, the gods of Olympus, took over in a bloody uprising. Many of the Titans, who lost, were banished to Tartarus, a Greek underworld. The ones who escaped this fate? The sea god Oceanus, and the all the females, who hadn't taken sides against their own children.

**Daddy Issues**

## Big Easy

There are actually more miles of canals in New Orleans than in Italy's watery playground, Venice.

**Crazy Canals**

## Favorite Games

The best-selling video game in history is *Minecraft*, with over 180 million copies sold, across platforms that range from Linux to smartphones.

**Dumb Phones**

## Bad Blood

Humans have red blood, but that's not the only color for blood in the animal kingdom. Spiders and octopuses bleed blue. Some worms bleed green, and some bleed violet. And many insects, like butterflies, have yellow blood.

**Rainbow Connection**

## Crazy Canals

In 1817, New York City had everything—except a good connection to the profitable commerce happening in the heartland of the country. So engineers built the Erie Canal in just eight short years, carving out a trench 40 feet wide and 4 feet deep, over the 363 miles between Buffalo and Albany, a route that took builders through forests and swamps and over literal cliffs. At multiple points, the canal had to cross existing rivers, elevated by aqueducts, and the final route included eighty-three locks to carry the canal over hills. Built mostly by American engineers who had never created anything like it before, it was the nation's largest civil engineering project to date—and under the leadership of New York governor DeWitt Clinton, it finished both early and under budget, perhaps for the last time in history. When it opened in 1825, the canal made New York City the most important port in the country overnight, firmly establishing it as a capital of the world and opening the American interior to far more rapid settlement.

**Crazy Swamps**
**Governor Clinton**

## Governor Clinton

Before he led construction of the Erie Canal, DeWitt Clinton served as mayor of New York City, where he commissioned the master plan for the city grid that, with surprisingly few changes, has become the actual map of New York. Even more remarkable, when the map was made, in 1811, the existing city barely reached north of Washington Square Park, at the southern tip of Manhattan. But Clinton's planners envisioned an orderly city that stretched hundreds of blocks, all the way up to the top of the island. The most significant change along the way: Clinton's original plan made no provision for all the city parks that now dot the grid.

**Famous Gridirons**
**City Parks**

## Mistaken Scientists

The theory of plate tectonics says that the earth is made of giant plates that slowly move in relationship to each other, creating earthquakes and mountains. But when German geophysicist Alfred Wegener came up with the idea in 1912, respectable geologists rejected the notion as hogwash. It took until the 1960s, when oceanic cartographer Marie Tharp created her groundbreaking maps of the ocean floor, for Wegener's idea to gain traction. Seismometers placed around the world to monitor nuclear testing that same decade sealed the deal: they showed that most of the world's active geologic features, like volcanoes and earthquakes, showed up along the boundaries of tectonic plates.

**Orderly Earthquakes**

## Rainbow Connection

Kermit the Frog's performance of "Rainbow Connection," from 1979's *The Muppet Movie*, may be the only song sung by a talking frog ever to hit the U.S. pop charts. It sat in the Billboard Top 40 for seven weeks—and nabbed an Academy Award nomination.

**Beloved Puppets**

## Daddy Issues

Nobody's sure how many children the Mongolian conqueror Genghis Khan had, but he seems to have had them just about everywhere he conquered. His official heirs ruled in eastern Europe, the Middle East, and China for over seven hundred years after his reign began in 1206—the last was deposed in 1920. But scientists estimate that one out of every two hundred people alive today is a direct descendant of Khan.

**Long Rains**

## Dumb Phones

We know Alexander Graham Bell as the inventor of the telephone. Elisha Gray, another inventor, filed a patent for his own telephonic creation only hours after Bell did. Bell's invention used a water microphone and a receiver suspiciously like ones developed earlier by Gray. But after wrangling in court for years, Bell finally won, and Gray switched careers, becoming a college professor.

**Underwater Sounds**

# Alien Sightings

The first UFOs in the United States were reported in the mid-1940s, but they weren't the first UFOs in history. During the time of Thutmose III, fiery disks were observed floating in ancient Egyptian skies.

**Signs and Wonders**

The Roman historian Livy reported phantom ships in the sky in the winter of 218 BC.

**Signs and Wonders**

Armies on both sides of a battle between Rome and Pontus reported seeing a giant flaming molten silver object fall from the sky in 74 BC.

**Signs and Wonders**

In 1561, papers in Nuremberg, Germany, reported that residents had seen hundreds of strange-shaped objects moving overhead and heard a giant crash outside the city.

**Big Crashes**

In 1917, thousands of Portuguese thought they saw the sun shake and fall from the sky in the district of Santarém.

**Signs and Wonders**

The number of global UFO sightings has climbed since 1990, when there were 319. By 2018, there were ten times as many: just over 3,700. But that's actually a drop from the highest number of UFO's ever reported: 8,696, in 2014. Why the drop in sightings? Nobody knows.

**Signs and Wonders**

In 1897, newspapers in both Dallas and Fort Worth received a report of a UFO crash, including the burial of the alien who had piloted it, near Aurora, Texas.

**Big Crashes**

A Baptist preacher claimed to have seen a crashed spacecraft, complete with expired aliens, in Missouri in 1941.

**Big Crashes**

## Crazy Swamps

South America's Pantanal is a tropical wetland almost ten times as big as the Everglades in Florida. It's also larger than over half of the individual states in America. Mostly in Brazil, the swamp also extends into Bolivia and Paraguay, and contains the most diverse collection of water plants in the world.

**Paraguay History**

## Famous Gridirons

St. Lawrence was treasurer of the Roman church in AD 258, when Emperor Valerian executed the sitting pope and demanded that Lawrence bring him all the church's treasures. Legend says Lawrence spent the next several days giving away all the church's money to the poor, then gathered people who were disabled and blind and brought them to the emperor, telling him, "These are the treasures of the church." Unamused, Valerian had Lawrence roasted to death on a red-hot gridiron. He became the patron saint of comedians when he reportedly quipped, "I'm done on this side, turn me over!"

**Missing Treasures**

## Beloved Puppets

The world's first puppets were probably made in Egypt, where figures with articulated arms and legs, made from ivory and clay, have been found in ancient tombs. And some researchers think that puppets took the stage even before human actors ever performed in plays.

**Ebony and Ivory**

## Orderly Earthquakes

For years, scientists believed that big quakes, like the 1906 monster that left early San Francisco a pile of fiery wreckage, were relatively infrequent. But new research shows that three big tremors rattled settlers to the area in the decades before the one that struck San Francisco: in 1838, 1865, and 1890—which may mean the next big one is coming sooner than we think.

**The Big One**

## City Parks

Frederick Law Olmsted is perhaps history's most beloved designer of city parks—but he wasn't when he won the contract for his most famous creation, New York City's Central Park. It was the thirty-six-year-old's very first gig.

**First Gigs**

## Long Rains

In the United States, the record for most consecutive days with rain goes to the Hawaiian island Oahu, with 331. But in Texas in the spring of 2007, it rained *without stopping* for 45 days straight. On the heels of a brutal drought, the continuous rainfall turned tiny creeks into 100-foot-wide rivers, washed away stores and homes, and dredged up fire ants and snakes from their underground homes.

**Crazy Ants**

## Underwater Sounds

Sound travels five times faster underwater than it does in air, and underwater, sound resonates directly in human facial bones, which means that human hearing extends to a higher range below the surface than above.

**Whale Songs**

## Paraguay History

The bloodiest international war in the Americas was fought against Paraguay. During the War of the Triple Alliance, Argentina, Brazil, and Uruguay signed a secret treaty, then went to war against Paraguay, which is just one-seventh the size of Argentina and one-twentieth the size of Brazil. Between 1864 and 1870, the conflict devastated Paraguay, where it's estimated that between 70 and 90 percent of the male population died in less than a decade.

**Triple Threat**

## Signs and Wonders

The chemical element neon was discovered in 1898, and it only took thirteen years for the first neon light to appear, in 1911. By the 1920s, neon signs were becoming a staple in advertising, spearheaded by the Packard car company. Pure neon, a colorless gas, naturally burns red when exposed to electricity. All the other colors come from the addition of other gases: orange from helium, green from krypton, lavender from argon, and blue from mercury.

**Mercury Rising**

## Big Crashes

The tallest building ever commercially demolished was New York's Singer Building, torn down in 1968 to make room for One Liberty Plaza, a new skyscraper. But the shortest-lived skyscraper may be Philadelphia's One Meridian Plaza, which stood for just over twenty-seven years, between 1972 and 1999, before being demolished to make way for a Ritz-Carlton property.

**Putting on the Ritz**

## Whale Songs

Whalers in the 1800s knew that whales sang songs, referring to them as "singers" in their logbooks. But it wasn't until the 1970s, when a record of humpback whale songs hit the market, that they became a pop-culture sensation. Only a handful of whale species sing, and within those, it's the males who sing the longest and most complex songs. But each whale doesn't just sing his own individual tune. Although whale songs change over time, at any given moment, male whales in any area all sing remarkably similar songs—sometimes in harmony with one another.

**Living in Harmony**

## Living in Harmony
## Ebony and Ivory

Recorded in 1982, "Ebony and Ivory" was a monster hit by two monster stars that had each dominated the previous decades of American music: the Beatles in the 1960s and Stevie Wonder in the 1970s. Paul McCartney wrote the song, but when it hit number one, it made Stevie Wonder the first solo artist ever to score number one hits in three straight decades.

**Wonder Woman**

## Putting on the Ritz

César Ritz started life as a Swiss peasant but came to Paris as a waiter and became one of the most famous hoteliers in the world, credited with inventing the modern luxury hotel experience— as well as the king-sized bed. But his world-class hospitality took a toll: he suffered a collapse in 1902, just four years after the Paris Ritz opened, and in the sixteen years from then until his death, he never returned to full-time work.

**Swiss Cheese**

# Missing Treasures

The last time anyone saw the Ark of the Covenant, which held the tablets that contained the Ten Commandments, was in 607 BC, when Babylonians killed over a million people during an attack on Jerusalem. Survivors fled, and when they returned, the Ark was gone.

**The Ten Commandments**

Visigoth king Alaric sacked Rome in 410 and headed south laden with loot, but died soon after. Legend says his troops diverted a river, buried their king and his loot in the riverbed, then let the river flow back over them, but the treasure has never been found.

**Big Rivers**

When Hernán Cortés appeared in Mexico in 1519, Montezuma, the Aztec emperor, greeted him with treasure, hoping it would make him go away. Instead, the Spanish sacked the city, until they were driven out by the Aztecs. Aztec legend says the retreating Spanish dumped untold treasure in Lake Texcoco, which Aztec forces retrieved and hid in another lake, in present-day Utah.

**State of Utah**

Colonel John Singleton Mosby and his Confederate raiders reportedly scored a bag full of gold, silver, and jewelry during an attack on Union general Edwin Stoughton. But when Union reinforcements showed up, Mosby gave two men orders to bury the stash somewhere in Fairfax County, Virginia. The men were killed before they could return, and Mosby, the only other witness, never collected the loot or gave up his secret. But that's not the only treasure lost in the Civil War: millions of dollars in gold went unaccounted for during the conflict.

## Be Civil

The Peking Man fossil, excavated in China in the 1920s, provided a crucial link in the evolutionary record of humankind, but it disappeared during World War II, perhaps sunk with the Japanese ocean liner *Awa Maru*, which went down while serving as a hospital ship in 1945, when an American submarine mistook it for a destroyer.

## Crucial Links

## Mercury Rising

Early attempts to measure temperature used water or alcohol in glass, but few of the devices, including one by Galileo, were very accurate. It wasn't until 1714 that the German scientist Daniel Gabriel Fahrenheit invented the mercury thermometer—and the scale of degrees that bears his name—with the temperature of the human body set at 100 degrees.

**Body Heat**

## Crazy Ants

Officially, the world's biggest ant colony stretches for 3,700 miles down the coast of the Mediterranean Sea, home to billions of Argentine ants. But there may be more to it: Argentine ants, native to South America, are now spread across the globe in a way that makes some scientists wonder if there's really only one giant mega-colony that stretches across the whole world.

**Excellent Climates**

## Body Heat

When Daniel Gabriel Fahrenheit invented the mercury thermometer in 1714, he believed the temperature of the human body was an even 100 degrees. But that temperature seems to be dropping. In 1851, when another German doctor measured the average body heat of 25,000 people, he got a result of 98.6 degrees Fahrenheit, which was corroborated several years later by data from Civil War soldiers. But a recent Stanford University study found that the average body temperature today is even lower: more like 97.5.

**Be Civil**

## Excellent Climates

California has relatively high temperatures, but Santa Barbara contains an unusual scrap of Mediterranean climate, due to its singular mix of water and mountains: Santa Barbara boasts the only peaks in the United States that lie along an east–west axis, which moderates the city's relatively cool, sunny weather, and have given it the reputation of an American Riviera.

**East Meets West**

## Triple Threat

The ancient Greek mathematician Pythagoras is still famous today because he gets credit for the theorem that calculates the relationship between the sides of a triangle. But it turns out, he may not even have written it. He was the leader of a group of mystical mathematicians who believed that numbers ruled the universe, and any one of them might have authored the text.

**Gangs of Mystics**

## First Gigs

Pope Francis, elected in 2013, worked a number of jobs before joining the Jesuits, including serving as a bouncer at a bar.

**Big Bounces**

## Swiss Cheese

In America, we call a cheese "Swiss" if it's full of holes. But actual cheesemakers in Switzerland work like crazy to keep holes out of their cheese—to them, it's the sign of an inferior product.

**Full of Holes**

## Wonder Woman

The creator of Wonder Woman, Dr. William Moulton Marston, also invented one of the world's first lie detectors, based on his observation as a doctor that people's blood pressure rose when they were lying.

**Blood Pressure**

## The Ten Commandments

Most religions based on the Hebrew Bible agree there are ten commandments in the book of Exodus—they just don't agree on what exactly those commandments are. Jewish tradition holds that the first few lines of the commandments, which describe God, are one command, followed by a second command, which is a warning against false gods. But Protestants and Greek Orthodox see that entire first section as Commandment #1.

**Church Traditions**

## Church Traditions

The original use of the term *devil's advocate* was recorded in 1760, in proceedings to decide whether a person was worthy to become a priest or not. The devil's advocate brought up all the candidate's flaws, while God's advocate stuck up for the candidate's good points.

**Bickering Priests**

## Be Civil

As the American Civil War was being fought, China's Qing dynasty was being torn apart by civil strife as well. Between 1850 and 1877, it's estimated that up to 100 million people died as a result of the conflicts in China, making it probably the deadliest period in all of history until then.

**East Meets West**

## The Big One

Californians aren't the only residents of an earthquake-prone zone who are bracing for the Big One. In the Tōkai region of Japan, which runs along the Pacific Ocean, models predict that a magnitude 8 quake is due to strike at the foot of Mount Fuji sometime soon. And Mount Fuji isn't just a potent national symbol: it's an active volcano.

**Ring of Fire**

## Crucial Links

Golfers who say they're "hitting the links" are harking back to the first days of golf, when it was invented in Scotland. In Old English, *hlinc* means "ridge" or "ground that rises," usually on coastal dunes—where golf was first played, in sight of the sea.

**Cool Dunes**

## East Meets West
## State of Utah

Utah's not exactly smack in the middle of the country—it's more like in the east of the west. But it's where two major east–west building projects met: the first transcontinental telegraph, which was joined together at Salt Lake City in 1861, and the transcontinental railroad, which joined at Utah's Promontory Point less than a decade later, in 1869. The first telegram that Western Union sent after the telegraph was completed was directed to President Abraham Lincoln from the chief justice of California, Stephen J. Field. The Civil War had broken out in April of that year, and Field's message wasn't a celebration of the forward march of progress into a Jetsonian future. Instead, it showed his concern for the endurance of the Union. His great hope for the telegraph, he wrote, was that it would help keep the country bound together and increase the loyalty of western states to the struggling Union.

## North–South

## North–South
## Big Rivers

The Mississippi River cuts north–south across the United States, from Minnesota to the Gulf of Mexico, for 2,340 miles, a distance that takes a single drop of water ninety days to travel. It's been home to both Native American and European cities for centuries, but it doesn't stay put itself. The river's current path is only a few hundred years old, and parts of it have already moved: on April 26, 1876, residents of the river town of Vicksburg, Mississippi, woke up to discover that the river had left town. Overnight, its course had shifted miles to the west. And it's probably not done yet: if the U.S. Army Corps of Engineers hadn't intervened, the Mississippi might already have carved out a new path that would bypass New Orleans, leaving that great river city without a river as well.

## Native American Cities

## Big Bounces

The bounciest ball in the world is the Super Ball, invented in 1964 by a chemist named Norman Stingley from a synthetic polymer he called Zectron. Baseballs barely bounce when dropped from waist height—but Super Balls bounce back up to 92 percent of the distance they fell—and shoot sky-high when they're hurled at the ground. Golf balls are also much more bouncy than baseballs—because they've got a rubber core hidden inside.

**Sky-High**

## Cool Dunes

Despite familiar images of African and Middle Eastern deserts, the world's biggest sand desert is actually in Australia: the Simpson Desert, whose red sands cover 65,000 miles of the country's interior, with dunes 100 miles long, and up to 130 feet high.

**G'day, Mate**

## Native American Cities

In AD 1250, the city built by the Mississippi people directly across the Mississippi River from modern-day St. Louis had a bigger population than the city of London at the time.

**Native American Roads**

## Blood Pressure

Think your blood pressure's high? A giraffe's heart has got to pump blood all the way up its 6-foot neck, so its normal blood pressure is 280/180: twice as high as humans, and among the highest in the world.

**Gentle Giants**

## Ring of Fire

Four-fifths of the world's seismic activity happens around the Pacific Ocean, where a string of almost five hundred volcanoes pop off around the region's tectonic plates, which are shoved under one another far more frequently than anywhere else on the globe.

**Stop Shoving**

## G'day, Mate

Along with Papua New Guinea, Australia is home to the world's only egg-laying mammals: the echidna and the platypus. The two of them form their own tiny subspecies of mammals: the monotremes. And the male platypus has a spur on each hind foot that excretes venom, making it the only venomous mammal in Australia.

**Pick Your Poison**

Twenty-one of the world's twenty-five most venomous snakes call Australia home.

**Pick Your Poison**

Half the world's legal opium is grown in Tasmania.

**Illegal Opium**

Perth is the most isolated city in the world, as measured by being the farthest from other major population centers. It's 1,300 miles away from Adelaide, the nearest city, with a population of over 100,000. But it's closer to the capital of Indonesia, Jakarta (about 1,850 miles away), than it is to Australia's capital, Sydney (2,100 miles away).

**Lost City**

Twenty percent of modern Australians are descended from convicts who were sent to the continent—and 74 percent of modern Tasmanians.

**Pesky Rabbits**

Australia boasts the largest cattle ranch in the world—bigger than the nation of Israel.

**Cowgirl Up**

## Gangs of Mystics
## Bickering Priests

In 1378, after the death of the reigning pope, Urban VI was elected to the church's top spot. Depending on whom you talk to, he turned out to be either a crazy jerk with a wild temper or an important reformer who told the ruling priests that they weren't allowed to use their power to make themselves rich. In any case, the cardinals who elected him started to regret it pretty much immediately. They elected a rival pope, Clement VII, only six months later—the first time the same college of cardinals had ever elected two popes at the same time. Urban VI did prove to have some brutal tendencies—after the execution of several cardinals who had run afoul of him, he complained that there wasn't enough screaming—but even after his death in 1389, the Great Schism didn't end. Backers of Urban VI just elected another pope in his place, and Europe lived with competing papacies for almost forty years, until both popes resigned and a third who refused to resign was excommunicated, and the church elected a brand-new pope, Martin V.

## Long Fights

## Sky-High

How high is the sky? Cloud cover disappears about 7.5 miles above Earth, but the atmosphere doesn't run out until 62 miles from the ground. And if you're in a plane, you're usually just above the cloud cover: between 6 and 7 miles up.

**Air Traffic**

## Lost City

In the heart of the Atlantic Ocean, between the coast of West Africa and North America, on the top of the underwater mountain known as the Atlantis Massif, sits a mysterious geologic feature unlike anything else on earth: a vast collection of 200-foot towers of white limestone, formed as giant chimneys for warm-water vents even deeper in the rock.

**Weird Beauty**

## Long Fights

The longest boxing match in history was seven hours and nineteen minutes, fought between 9:00 p.m. and 4:00 a.m. in New Orleans, in 1893. The big kicker: no one won. Both boxers got so tired that the bout ended by decision, with a determination of "no contest."

**So Tired**

## Gentle Giants

Baby elephants stay in the womb more than twice as long as human babies, with a gestation period of eighteen to twenty-two months. Once they're born, they drink as much as 3 gallons of their mother's milk per day. And they suck their trunks—just like human babies suck their thumbs.

**Unusual Pets**

### Air Traffic

At any given time, there are about ten thousand planes in the sky, carrying about 1.25 million people.

**On the Road**

## Native American Roads On the Road

Many U.S. roads, from city streets to interstates, started out as Native American trails, including Vermont's Route 22A and Brooklyn's Atlantic Avenue.

**Maple Syrup**

## Stop Shoving

The small Arctic rodents known as lemmings are the subject of a number of crazy myths. Because lemmings travel in large groups, some early naturalists concluded that they must fall from the sky en masse. And legend also held that if the little guys got angry enough, they'd explode. But the most enduring myth about lemmings—that they blindly follow one another, to the point of leaping off cliffs in larger herds—was a fraud perpetuated by Disney filmmakers in 1958's *White Wilderness*, when they deliberately shoved dozens of lemmings off a cliff to get a dramatic shot.

**Fearless Assassins**

## Illegal Opium

In the late 1600s, China opened to trade with Europe after the closure of the Silk Road hundreds of years before. Europe had an insatiable demand for Chinese goods, but the Chinese weren't nearly as interested in stuff from Europe. So to make up the trade deficit, the British East In dia Company started to export illegal opium to China in the late 1700s, creating over ten million opium addicts. The emperor banned the drug in 1810, but by 1839, almost 30 percent of all the men in China were addicted to opium. China complained to Queen Victoria, asking her to stop the trade, then confiscated over a thousand tons of English opium and started locking up opium dealers when they got no response. Not long after, English ships broke through a Chinese blockade of the Pearl River, setting off a series of naval battles won by England's superior navy—which led to Hong Kong being deeded to England in perpetuity as an English trading base.

## Poison Poppies

## Full of Holes

Sinkholes form when water washes away soft stones or salt way below ground, and the crust of the earth above suddenly caves in. They've swallowed moving buses full of people, entire homes, and whole city blocks. But the biggest one in the world is in a forest in China. It's over 2,100 feet deep, with a second hole that collapsed in the bottom of the first—and a waterfall within.

**Crazy Waterfalls**

## Poison Poppies

The field of poison poppies that Dorothy fell asleep in during *The Wizard of Oz* probably wouldn't have killed her—no real poppies give off poisonous fumes like the ones author L. Frank Baum invented. But in the movie version, the on-set "snow" that killed off the poppies probably wasn't great for Dorothy—it was made of asbestos.

**Pick Your Poison**

# Pick Your Poison

Cyanide's a famous poison, but you actually absorb it all the time. In fact, your body turns compounds in rice, wheat, sugar, soy, almonds, and lima beans into cyanide when it metabolizes them.

**Gross Beans**

The entire hemlock plant, from its white blossoms to its carrot-shaped root, is poisonous. It causes paralysis, most importantly of the respiratory system: the cause of death for Socrates.

**Ancient Teachers**

Strychnine is widely used as a rat poison. It also causes respiratory paralysis—and once you've taken it, there's no cure.

**Too Many Rats**

Curare is a potent mix of South American ingredients that causes paralysis of the respiratory system—but not the heart. So victims lose their ability to talk or move, but are still wide awake. That sounds terrible, but there's a bright side—if you can get a buddy to give you mouth-to-mouth resuscitation for long enough, the poison will begin to work out of your system, and you may survive.

**Best Buddies**

Arsenic's actually a pretty useful chemical compound, which occurs naturally in volcanic ash, and with copper and gold deposits. It can be used to kill insects, preserve wood, and cure syphilis. But taken in large doses, it causes stomach pain, nausea, convulsions—and death. And it was a favorite of medieval poisoners because those are the same symptoms as cholera—a prolific natural killer at the time.

**Kicking Cholera**

## Pesky Rabbits

Bugs Bunny started life as a duck. Warner Bros. was in a hurry to make a new cartoon and had just introduced Daffy Duck the year before, in 1937. So under time pressure, artists repurposed some leftover Daffy Duck jokes and scenarios, put Bugs in Daffy's place—and a star was born.

**Fake Animals**

## Cowgirl Up

Cowboys get most of the press, but the Wild West was full of women who could also rope a steer, ride a horse, and shoot. They participated in early rodeos and Wild West shows, and one of them, Mabel Strickland, beat out men to win multiple steer-roping competitions in the 1920s. But when the first professional rodeo group, the Cowboy Turtle Association, formed in 1936, women weren't allowed to compete in the biggest events.

**Lady Samurai**

## Ancient Teachers

The next time you see an inspirational quote from Seneca on the internet, take it with a grain of salt—his most famous student was the infamous Roman emperor Nero, who probably killed his mother and stepbrother, although there's no proof that he actually fiddled while Rome burned.

**Fast Burning**

## So Tired

In 1965, a high school student named Randy Gardner set the still-unbroken world record for staying awake, as part of a science fair experiment. He went without sleeping for 264 hours, or eleven days. Even after not sleeping for eight to ten days, most humans return to normal functioning after a day or two of normal sleep. But lab rats that are kept awake for longer than two weeks always die.

**Too Many Rats**

## Fast Burning

During a grandmaster game, chess champions burn up to 6,000 calories and can lose as many as 10 pounds while sitting still—because of all the energy they burn in their brains.

**High Voltage**
**Checkmate**

## Weird Beauty

Peacocks originated around the Indian subcontinent, but their beauty is so striking that they've been a sought-after pet since ancient times. They were given as a gift to King Solomon and carried west in caravans, arriving in Greece by around 500 BC. Ancient Romans loved them for their vivid colors, and they appeared in England around AD 300. The first peacocks to reach the United States actually landed in Hawaii in 1860, and since then, they've created their own populations, not dependent on human help, all over the Hawaiian islands.

**Unusual Pets**

## Maple Syrup

To make 1 gallon of maple syrup, you need 40 gallons of sap—and each tree only produces about 10 gallons of sap per season.

**Canadian Bacon**

## Fearless Assassins

What's the difference between a samurai and a ninja? A samurai belonged to a class of Japanese military nobility. Ninjas were martial artists, trained in everything from espionage to meteorology.

**Awesome Ninjas**
**Lady Samurai**

## Crazy Waterfalls

Cameron Falls, in Alberta, Canada, flows clear most days. But heavy rains stir up an underlying sedimentary rock called argillite in the riverbed, which turns the whole thing bright pink.

**Thinking Pink**

## Fake Animals

For years after the first duck-billed platypus specimens reached Europe, Europeans insisted they must be fake, sewn together out of the parts of other animals.

**Sewing Machines**

## Gross Beans

Why do we fart when we eat beans? They've got sugars in them that our bodies don't easily digest, and when that sugar comes into contact with our gut bacteria, gas is created.

**Gut Bacteria**

## Too Many Rats

Rats are originally from northern China, but they're now present in every city in the world—except for the entire province of Alberta, Canada, which has no significant population of rats due to lucky geography and aggressive anti-rat programs.

**Canadian Bacon**

# Kicking Cholera

Cholera is one of the deadliest diseases in history, and it hasn't been wiped out by modern medicine: 120,000 people still die of it each year. But the cure is simple: no matter how severe a case, you'll probably survive if you stay hydrated, which is easier said than done with a disease that gives you both diarrhea and nausea.

**Stay Hydrated**

# Best Buddies

Marilyn Monroe and Ella Fitzgerald became friends after Monroe went to see Fitzgerald sing in 1954. At the time, the owner of L.A.'s best club didn't want to book Fitzgerald, because he said she wasn't glamorous enough. So Monroe offered a deal: book Fitzgerald, and Monroe would sit in the front row for every show. When the club owner agreed, Fitzgerald's fans snapped up tickets so fast that he added an extra week to her run—and the First Lady of Song never had to play small clubs again.

**Famous Nightclubs**

# Checkmate

Nobody's sure who invented chess, but it appeared in India around AD 500 and migrated through the Middle East to Europe as the Islamic Empire expanded. One legend says it was created by a Chinese military commander, Han Xin, to commemorate an actual battle he took part in—then became popular in China as the Elephant Game before it was taken up in India and Persia. Another says that it was invented by a wise Indian man to teach a harsh king the importance of all his subjects.

**Board Games**

The standard chess set didn't become standard until the 1800s.

**Board Games**

The term *checkmate* comes from the Persian phrase *shah mat*, which means "The king is helpless."

**Board Games**

There are more possible games of chess ($10^{120}$) than electrons in the universe ($10^{79}$).

**Board Games**

Chess is one of the world's most enduring games, but it's run afoul of almost every religion: varieties of the game have been banned by the Eastern Orthodox Church, Catholics, Puritans, Muslims, rabbis, and the Knights Templar.

**Board Games**

Globally, about 600 million people know how to play chess today.

**Board Games**

## High Voltage

The first electric street lighting was created by arc lamps that used huge amounts of alternating current (AC), that buzzed and threw off light as it jumped between a pair of carbon elements. The lamps were so loud, and so dangerous, that they could only be used outdoors, and dozens of people died in accidents with them. Edison's idea was to use direct current (DC), at a much lower voltage, to make electric light safe for people's homes. Edison did everything he could to discredit AC power, including playing up the role it played in deaths by execution. But he may have won the war simply by choosing the right neighborhood to electrify: he placed his first-ever power plant on Pearl Street in New York City, where it could light up homes of some of the most powerful tastemakers anywhere in the country.

## Flashing Lights

## Awesome Ninjas

Real ninjas were so good at keeping secrets that historians know very little about them. They seem to have been farmers who operated in the mountains of Japan in the late 1400s until the turn of the next century, working as guerrilla fighters and assassins. But much of what we think we know about them was written decades later—perhaps because their contemporaries thought recording their exploits might not be quite safe.

**Mountain People**

## Lady Samurai

All samurai clans welcomed *onna-bugeisha*, or "women warriors"—and they were surprisingly common. At the battle of Senbon Matsubaru, fought in 1580, thirty-five of about a hundred fallen fighters were female, according to archaeological evidence.

**Thinking Pink**

## Thinking Pink

Back in the day, pink wasn't a color for girls: boy and girl babies both wore white. Pink first became fashionable among Europeans in the 1700s as a sign of luxury. And it was favored first in garb for little boys, because it was a variant of red, which people saw as a military, and therefore masculine, color.

**Military Uniforms**

## Gut Bacteria

Our stomachs contain ten times as many microbes as there are cells in our bodies. The tiny organisms help us gain energy from food, impact our immune system and metabolism, and even help us make serotonin—the hormone that causes happiness.

**Crazy Hormones**

## Unusual Pets

In the 1700s and 1800s, colonial America's pet of choice was the squirrel, and not just on the pioneer fringes of the young nation. Squirrels were widely available in urban markets, and rich kids paraded them around fancy homes on gold leashes.

**King Midas**

## Sewing Machines
## Military Uniforms

French tailor Barthélemy Thimonnier invented the first working sewing machine and used it to land a contract sewing uniforms for the French Army, but his fellow tailors were so worried he'd put them out of business they burned down his factory. He won prizes for his invention at several world's fairs and kept filing new patents on it for a decade, but wound up returning to his life as a tailor and dying in poverty.

**Up in Smoke**

## Canadian Bacon

Don't try ordering Canadian bacon in Canada. The popular breakfast food of unsmoked cured pork loin that Americans call Canadian bacon is most commonly known as "back bacon" in Canada.

**Serious About Breakfast**

## Stay Hydrated

Dehydration's no joke: when we go for too long without water, we can wind up with kidney problems, have seizures, and go into shock. But weirdly, we might not be all that thirsty, even when we're very dehydrated. Other signs to watch for include fatigue, confusion, crying without tears—and bad breath.

**Halitosis** ■■■■■■■■■■■■■■■■■■■■■■■

## Famous Nightclubs

CBGB was a biker bar until late 1973, when Hilly Kristal reopened it as a home for country, bluegrass, and blues. But one of the first acts Kristal booked, Squeeze, had members who would become part of seminal punk acts like Television and the Patti Smith Group, and when another indie venue closed that summer, punk bands began to flood CBGB's stage, turning it into the epicenter of the New York punk scene.

**Bluegrass** ■■■■■■■■■■■■■■■■

## Bluegrass

Bluegrass isn't actually blue, but a darker shade of green than the standard American lawn. But blue oat grass is a true steely blue. And little bluestem grass, although it's greenish gray and not blue, turns colors in the fall just like the leaves of a tree: to orange, red, and purple.

**National Pastime**

## Crazy Hormones

Oxytocin is the hormone our brains release when we feel love—but it also has the power to help wounds heal, by reducing swelling in the body.

**Love Is a Drug**

## Halitosis

The term *halitosis* is just a fancy way of saying bad breath. (*Halitus* is Latin for "breath.") The word was invented in 1874 by a doctor who used it in his book about the breath, but the reason you probably know it today is because Listerine popularized it in a 1920s marketing campaign, and when dentists started using the term, Listerine sales took off.

**Deep Breath**

## National Pastime

Carnivals started out as a Christian religious tradition: a last-hurrah festival before going into the forty-day fasting season of Lent, perhaps named from the Latin *carnelevarium*, which means to leave out meat, and with possible roots in Roman pagan festivals. But although the carnival tradition is ancient, the traveling carnival with the lighted midway didn't start up until the Chicago World's Fair, in 1893. On the far border of the grounds was the Midway Plaisance, full of games, burlesque, and freak shows—along with the world's first Ferris wheel. Shortly after the World's Fair, Otto Schmitt formed a company to take thirteen sideshow acts on the road. In grand carnival fashion, it almost immediately went bust. But members of his company started their own, and the crowds loved the magic of the midway. By 1902, there were seventeen carnival companies in the United States, with forty-six by 1905. By 1937, that number had swelled to over three hundred. The carnival midway had become a household name, and the traveling fair had become a national pastime.

**Bit of Burlesque** ▬▬▬▬▬▬

## King Midas

King Midas is known in Greek mythology for praying that everything he touched would turn to gold—and dying of starvation when his prayer was answered. Less well-known: his father, Gordias, is the namesake of the Gordian knot. Legend has it that their native Phrygia was without a king until an oracle said the next man to enter the city in an oxcart should be crowned. The lucky winner was the farmer Gordias, who was the first to show up with a cart and some oxen. His son, Midas, dedicated the cart to the gods and tied it up with an incredibly intricate knot that became the source of another legend: whoever could unravel it would rule all Asia. Years later, Alexander the Great couldn't figure out Midas's knot—so he hacked it to pieces, and went on to conquer the world.

**Cut Loose**

## Up in Smoke

In 1666, most of London, which was composed of cramped wooden homes and stores, went up in flames during the days-long Great Fire, ignited after the king's baker failed to completely extinguish the coals in his oven. Thousands were left homeless, but the fire had a bright side: it burned up many of the rats that carried fleas infected with the plague. With the disappearance of the fleas, England's last major outbreak of the bubonic plague—which had been raging since 1665—ended.

**Flea Traps Burnt Out**

## Deep Breath

Humans can hold their breath longer under cold water than in warm water, because a diving reflex slows our heart and metabolism. So the world records for breath-holding have been set by free divers, who descend deep into freezing water. The record to date was achieved by the German diver Tom Sietas, who didn't breathe for twenty-two minutes and twenty-two seconds, most of which he spent deep in chilly waters.

**Weird Reflexes**

# Mountain People

What were the famous warring clans of the Hatfields and McCoys so mad about? Apparently, the whole feud started with a single pig. Pigs weren't cheap in their poor region, on the Kentucky and West Virginia border. So when a Hatfield was accused of stealing a McCoy's pig, it was a big deal. When that Hatfield got off in a trial that seemed to be thrown by the star witness, the McCoys were outraged. And when that star witness was killed by a pair of McCoys two years later, a feud erupted. It didn't help when the son of the Hatfield clan patriarch got a McCoy girl pregnant—and then dumped her for her cousin. Two years later, a brawl between Hatfields and McCoys at a local election ended with the death of a Hatfield. The guilty McCoys were arrested, but angry Hatfields kidnapped them from the police and killed all three. Twenty Hatfields were charged—but not one was arrested. On New Year's Day in 1888, the Hatfields attacked the home of McCoy patriarch Randolph McCoy. He escaped, but his son and daughter were killed, and his wife's skull was crushed. A few days later, a bounty hunter captured nine Hatfield supporters, and the case went all the way to the U.S. Supreme Court—and ended with guilty verdicts against all nine Hatfields.

**Use Your Words**

## Bit of Burlesque

A modern burlesque patron walking into a Victorian burlesque hall might get a bit of a shock: at the time, "exotic dancers" were usually fully clothed, with comic elements to their costumes, like a woman wearing a horse's head or sequined armor. That's more true to the name than the modern incarnation: *burlesque* stems from the Italian word *burla*, for "joke."

**Prime Horseflesh**

## Board Games

The classic kids' board game Chutes and Ladders is an ancestor of Candy Land. They're both games where you jump ahead or fall back based on pure chance. But the roots of Chutes and Ladders go back even further. A version emerged in India as early as 200 BC, as part of religious lessons on the uncertainty of life. The game first reached Europe in 1892, via England, and Milton Bradley introduced it to U.S. audiences in 1943.

**Pure Chance**

## Love Is a Drug

When we fall in love, our brain's levels of serotonin, dopamine, and norepinephrine go sky-high—just like they do after a hit of cocaine.

**Drug Dealers** ▬▬▬▬▬▬▬▬▬▬▬▬▬▬▬▬▬▬

## Use Your Words

English may have one of the highest word counts in the world, with between a quarter and half a million words, depending on how you count, compared to less than half that number in French or German. But you don't need all of them to get your point across. If you learn only the most frequently used eight hundred words, you'll still understand about 75 percent of what's going on.

**Pardon My French** ▬▬▬▬▬▬▬▬▬▬▬▬▬▬

## Flea Traps

Fleas accelerate incredibly quickly when they jump: twenty times faster than a space shuttle. And they can jump incredibly high relative to their size: the equivalent of a human being able to leap a building with thirty stories.

**Flying Machines** ▬▬▬▬▬▬▬▬▬▬▬▬▬▬

## Cut Loose

The guillotine got famous during the French Revolution, but Germans had created a beheading device as early as the Middle Ages, and the English Halifax gibbet, which also featured an ax that slid, is so old no one knows who invented it. • • •

**Big Knives**

Dr. Joseph-Ignace Guillotin was trying to do condemned people a favor by pressing the French government for a more humane form of execution and was horrified when the death machine became known by his name. • • • • • • • • • • •

**Pardon My French**

Not everyone tramped dolefully up the steps to their beheading—during the French Revolution, some victims of the guillotine took the opportunity to shout defiantly at the gathered crowds—and more than one guillotine victim danced their way to their deaths. • • • • • • • •

**Dance Parties**

In the 1790s, pint-sized guillotines were a popular toy for French kids, who used them to decapitate dolls and even small animals.

**Weird Toys**

French families of means sometimes had an unusual method of slicing bread and vegetables at dinner: tabletop guillotines.

**Eat Your Vegetables**

Executioners became celebrities during the French Revolution, with onlookers critiquing their speed and grace, especially in the tricky work of dispatching multiple victims.

**Unlikely Celebrities**

The guillotine persisted as a means of capital punishment in France until 1977.

**Pardon My French**

## Serious About Breakfast

Seventy-five percent of the maple syrup in the world comes from Quebec, where it's such big business that the Federation of Québec Maple Syrup Producers stashes away strategic reserves all over the province.

**Expensive Food**

## Drug Dealers

Snake oil got a bad name from shady salesmen in the 1800s, but it has genuine medicinal properties as an anti-inflammatory, because of its high omega-3 content. It probably arrived in the United States along with Chinese workers who helped build the transcontinental railroad, for their end-of-day aches and pains.

**Interesting Medicine**

## Burnt Out

The Centralia coal mine, in Pennsylvania, has been burning underground since 1962, through a deposit of coal that's 8 miles long. At its current rate, it could keep burning for another 250 years.

**Old Kohl**

## Weird Reflexes

Hiccups are a spasm of the diaphragm, brought on by eating or drinking too fast—especially carbonated beverages or spicy foods—or just by gulping too much air. Most cases go away after a few minutes—but in 1922, a young man named Charles Osborne got the longest-lasting case of hiccups on record. They started while he was in the process of slaughtering a hog, probably because of a burst blood vessel in his brain, and lasted for sixty-eight years. But with the help of doctors at the Mayo Clinic, Osborne learned to hide the sound with methodical breathing. He fathered eight kids with two wives—one of whom married him *after* he'd already begun his marathon spate of hiccups. And without explanation, his hiccups stopped a year before he died—giving him a brief respite before he passed away at ninety-seven.

**Spicy Foods** ▬▬▬▬▬▬

## Old Kohl

Men in ancient Babylon used kohl—a dark, powdery cosmetic—to color their nails, with rich folks favoring black and less wealthy using green. They also used manicure tools made from solid gold. • • • • • • •

**Fancy Fingerwork**

India was the home of the first known manicures, almost five thousand years ago, using henna, a plant-derived dye, to color the nails. But the first representations of pedicures are on Egyptian tombs. • • • • • • •

**Fancy Fingerwork**

In the fourteenth century, Chinese people began to mix egg whites, dye, and beeswax to create a rainbow of colored varnishes. Part of the point of having long nails: to indicate that the wearer was rich enough not to do manual labor. • • • • • • • • •

**Fancy Fingerwork**

The first nail salon in America was opened in 1878 by Mary Cobb, the wife of a podiatrist who had earned a fortune on foot powders and cosmetics. Legend has it that Cobb learned the secrets of the manicure in France, but she also introduced new elements to the process, including soaking the fingers. Her price: $1.25, or about $32.55 in today's money.

**Fancy Fingerwork**

When the automobile became popular in the 1920s, women started to apply the high-gloss auto paints to their nails. So in 1932, Revlon caught the hint and introduced a line of nail polishes in drugstores.

**Fancy Fingerwork**

## Big Knives

On their raids of Europe, which started in the 700s, elite Vikings carried incredibly well-made swords with them—so strong and sharp that Europeans didn't make their match until the Industrial Revolution. So scholars suspect the Scandinavian warriors may have imported the steel from more advanced Islamic metalworkers, or perhaps from carbon-rich German ore.

**Stockholm Syndrome**

## Pure Chance

Wilbur Wright won the first try at taking off in the flying machine the Wright brothers had built, in a coin toss. But the plane stalled after Wilbur's takeoff. So it was Orville, several days later, who was the first brother to take flight.

**Flying Machines**

## Stockholm Syndrome

The phrase *Stockholm syndrome*, which describes cases where a captive begins to identify with a captor, comes from a 1973 bank robbery in the Swedish capitol, when the hostages taken by the bank robbers told authorities they trusted their captors and were afraid they'd be killed if police intervened.

**Bank Robbery**

## Flying Machines

Leonardo da Vinci famously designed a flying machine at the dawn of the Renaissance, but he wasn't the only inventor to tinker with the idea in the four hundred years before the Wright brothers launched the first successful flight. Other attempts included an aerial steam carriage, a steam-jet dart, a military kite, a hand-powered airship, and mechanical birds. But Leonardo was still centuries before his time—most of these only appeared in the century before the Wright brothers finally succeeded in giving humanity wings.

**Bird Parts**

## Bird Parts

Birds have three eyelids: an upper lid that closes on a lower lid during sleep, just like humans—but also a clear third eyelid that closes *horizontally*, from side to side of the eye. It protects the bird's eye from dust and wind in flight, kind of like a pair of aviator goggles.

**Big Birds**

## Pardon My French

Swearing might be good for you: it seems to lead to higher trust between teams and increases your tolerance for pain. And humans aren't the only primates who do it: chimps that learn sign language start using the sign for *dirty* in exactly the same way humans use swear words.

**Angry Monkeys**

## Spicy Foods
## Expensive Food

During the days of Marco Polo, black pepper, which had to be imported to Europe from India and Asia, was worth the same amount per weight as silver.

**Eat Your Vegetables**

## Big Birds

A penguin species that went extinct at least 33 million years ago, *Anthropornis nordenskjoldi*, stood almost six feet tall.

**Big Cats**

## Angry Monkeys

How do you know if a monkey is angry? Watch out if it seems to be smiling! To monkeys, baring teeth is a sign of aggression, and if you smile back, they can get the signal that you're spoiling for a fight.

**No Smiling**

# Prime Horseflesh

The Triple Crown is composed of America's three premier horse races: the Kentucky Derby, the Preakness, and the Belmont Stakes. The Kentucky Derby is the world's most prestigious race for three-year old horses, because Kentucky is home to some of the best horse breeders in the world. Louisville built racetracks specifically for horses when informal horse races through the middle of town started to get out of hand.

**Old Hat**

The Preakness, run at Baltimore's Pimlico track, is the shortest of the Triple Crown races. It's named after the first horse ever to win the Dinner Party Stakes at Pimlico in 1870, the year it opened.

**Dinner Parties**

The Belmont Stakes is the oldest of the Triple Crown races, and the longest, named after the financier August Belmont, and run on a track just outside New York City.

**Dollar Signs**

## Dollar Signs

The slashed-S symbol for the U.S. dollar probably comes from the Spanish peso, the favorite coin for international trade after the Spanish minted large quantities from New World silver. Merchants wrote them up with an overlapped S and P. Then the curve of the P disappeared—and the dollar sign was born.

**Minty Fresh** ▬▬▬▬▬

## Eat Your Vegetables

Broccoli has more protein per calorie than steak.

**High Stakes** ▬▬▬▬▬

## Weird Toys

In ancient Egypt, kids spun grapevine wreaths around their waists. Medieval Europeans twirled wood hoops, and their gyrations looked so much like traditional Hawaiian hula that British sailors named the hoops after the dance.

**Grapevines** ▬▬▬▬▬

## Bank Robbery
## Fancy Fingerwork

Adam Worth was one of the most prolific bank robbers of all time, working in the decades just after the American Civil War with his partner, a ne'er-do-well rich kid known as Piano Charley, whose fingers were so sensitive that he could break an old-fashioned combination lock just by sensing the variations in weight as its tumblers spun. Worth masterminded bank heists around the globe, but he probably pulled off his most famous theft all on his own: stealing an incredibly famous portrait of the Duchess of Devonshire from an English gallery. He traveled with it for years, perhaps because it reminded him of a pretty barmaid named Kitty, who he and Piano Charley had both fallen in love with in their youth. Worth used it as a bargaining chip in his negotiations with the Pinkertons when he finally decided to surrender after a lifetime on the run.

**Famous Portraits**

## Famous Portraits
## Unlikely Celebrities

Lisa Gherardini was the wife of a fifteenth-century Florentine silk merchant, and the mother of five. But little else is known about her life, other than the fact that she served as the model for Leonardo da Vinci's *Mona Lisa*. Unfinished at his death, the portrait's now one of the most famous paintings in the world. Since it went up on the walls of Paris's Louvre Museum in 1815 (after four years in Napoleon's personal bedroom), it's drawn millions of admirers, some carrying flowers and poems. When the painting was stolen from the gallery in 1911, Parisians flooded the Louvre to gaze at the empty space where the image had hung. Today, the painting still provokes so many love letters that the Louvre has given Lisa her own post office box.

### Silk Worms

## Big Cats

Tigers' stripes aren't just on their fur—their skin is striped, too. And no two tigers have the same stripes—just like human fingerprints. •

**Finger Printing**

Depending on the breed, tigers can weigh between 300 and 650 pounds. But they've been known to eat over 80 pounds of meat in a single meal.•

**Dinner Parties**

Cats are famous for hating water, but tigers are great swimmers, swimming as much as 18 miles a day while they rove their domain.•

**Earn Your Stripes**

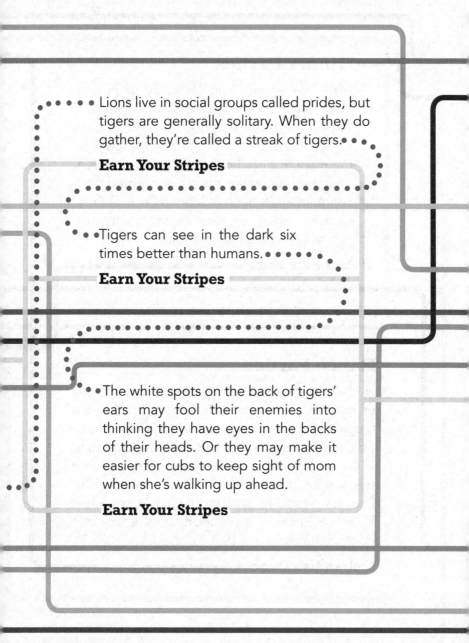

Lions live in social groups called prides, but tigers are generally solitary. When they do gather, they're called a streak of tigers.

**Earn Your Stripes**

Tigers can see in the dark six times better than humans.

**Earn Your Stripes**

The white spots on the back of tigers' ears may fool their enemies into thinking they have eyes in the backs of their heads. Or they may make it easier for cubs to keep sight of mom when she's walking up ahead.

**Earn Your Stripes**

## Dinner Parties

Marie de' Medici and Henry IV of France celebrated their wedding in 1600 with a fifty-course meal for three hundred guests. But perhaps the most memorable part of the meal occurred before anyone had even tasted a bite: when guests discovered that songbirds had been hidden in each of their napkins, ready to take flight the instant guests undid the intricate folds.

**Intricate Folds**

## Dance Parties

In 1347, hundreds of people danced in the streets of Aachen, Germany, until they collapsed—the biggest of the seemingly involuntary mass dances that swept Europe from the 1300s to around 1700. During outbreaks, bridges collapsed under the weight of dancers, children danced miles from town to town, and dancing monks perished from exhaustion. But nobody's sure why the dancing started—or why it stopped.

**Outlandish Dances**

## No Smiling

Legend has it that people didn't smile in old photographs because the exposure was so long that facial expressions might blur as they shifted. But that's only half the story: early photographers were trying to imitate painted portraits, which rarely showed smiling subjects because the expression was so hard to capture in paint. And some of it was sheer snobbery: Victorians and Edwardians both thought smiling was in bad taste.

**Bad Taste**

## High Stakes

In 2013, the professional boxer Floyd Mayweather earned more than any other athlete in the world, so he could afford to be one of the world's biggest gamblers. He wagered $5.9 million that the Indiana Pacers would lose out to the Miami Heat that year—and raked in a cool $6.5 million when they did.

**Hot Water**

## Outlandish Dances

Whirling dervish ceremonies, in which mystics spin in a ritual dance, were started by the thirteenth-century Persian poet Rumi, and then spread throughout the Ottoman Empire.

**Comfy Furniture**

## Old Hat

Panama hats have never been manufactured in Panama. They're made in Ecuador, and known as toquilla or Montecristi hats throughout Latin America today.

**White Hats**

## Grapevines

Most wine is made from a very specific species of grapes, *Vitis vinifera*. That's because they naturally contain the perfect blend of sugar, tannins, and acids to stay tasty after fermentation—unlike the vast majority of other fruits.

**First Fruits**

## First Fruits

The first fruit cultivated by humankind was probably the fig, which archaeological evidence shows was grown in Jericho over eleven thousand years ago—far earlier than people tamed grapes, oranges, or apples.

### First Flowers

## White Hats
## Intricate Folds

The traditional white French chef's hat has exactly one hundred folds, which legend says represents a hundred different ways to cook an egg.

### Counting Chickens

## Minty Fresh

Mint gets its name from the Greek nymph Minthe, whose domain is the river that flows through the underworld. According to legend, Hades, the god of the underworld, had a crush on her, so his consort had her turned into a minty plant.

### Bad Taste

## First Flowers

The first plants on the planet weren't flowers but conifers and ferns, according to the fossil record. But today, perhaps because they're so popular with humans, there are twenty times more flowering plants on the planet than ferns or conifers.

**Popular with Humans** ▬▬▬

## Earn Your Stripes

In Europe in the Middle Ages, stripes were a sign of disgrace, worn by prostitutes and clowns. Americans started using striped clothing for prisoners in the 1800s so that they'd be easy to recognize if they escaped. One other class of people who wore them: French sailors, whose striped shirts made it easy for them to spot their fellows who had fallen overboard. It was only when hip kids started wearing those now-iconic blue-and-white tops in the 1950s that stripes came into fashion.

**Stuck at Sea** ▬▬▬

## Bad Taste

Denatonium benzoate, a compound marketed under the name Bitrex, is so bitter and long-lasting that putting a fraction of a pound of it in a ton of rice makes it so nauseating no one can eat it. Today, it's used to keep kids safe by making dangerous household chemicals like antifreeze and detergent taste awful—so they're not tempted to swallow them.

**How Sweet It Is**

## Popular with Humans

The Victorian mania for collecting orchids started by accident. A British naturalist, William John Swainson, stuffed unbloomed orchids, which he thought of as junk, as packing material around other samples he'd collected to send back to England. But they bloomed on arrival, setting off a collecting craze that led to the horrific deaths of many orchid hunters—who ventured into tropical forests of South America and the South Pacific in search of the elusive blooms—and fortunes for a lucky few.

**Hidden Talents**

## Hidden Talents

Flowers don't have ears, but they can hear. When primroses pick up the sound of buzzing bees, their nectar becomes sweeter within just minutes.

**How Sweet It Is**

## Silk Worms

Legend has it that silk was discovered when a silk moth cocoon fell into the tea of the empress Lei Zu, who noticed delicate silk thread as the cocoon unwound. For centuries, the Chinese were the only people in the world who knew how to produce silk, with ingenious methods like feeding silkworms only white mulberry leaves to create white thread. But today, the most desirable worms for creating silk no longer have a wild population: they've been domesticated for so long that the species has lost the ability to fly.

**Fall Leaves**

# Finger Printing

You might think that a human fingerprint would have more in common with a chimp's than a koala bear's, but koala fingerprints are so close to human that it's not easy even for experts to tell the difference—which could make a koala bear a great accomplice if you're planning a big heist. Another reason not to trust koalas: they're not actually bears. They're marsupials, closer cousins to the kangaroo than the grizzly.

**Cute Chimps**

# Counting Chickens

Chickens can remember as many as a hundred different faces—of other chickens. Maybe because they live in a highly stratified social structure, where everyone knows their place.

**Ruling Class**

# How Sweet It Is

Pre-sugar, Europe, Asia, and Africa all got their sweet tooth satisfied by honey from bees, which are native to all three continents. But because the Americas didn't have bees, their sweets were made from fruit, tree sap, or—in the southwest—agave nectar.

**Honey Bees**

Sugarcane is native to New Guinea, the first place to cultivate it—originally just so people could chew on the sweet pulp.

**Big Islands**

The process of refining sugar was developed in India, where the earliest record of sugar mills were recorded, around AD 100. The Greeks found out about sugar a couple hundred years later, on visits to India.

**Innovations of India**

Around AD 500, Jundi Shapur, a Persian university, became the world's first teaching hospital, and also improved on the process of refining sugar—so it could be used as a medicine.

## Interesting Medicine

The Arabs blended ground almonds and sugar around AD 650 to create marzipan, which became a staple at elite feasts. Sugar spread through the Mediterranean via Arab military conquests and reached Europe with soldiers returning from the Crusades—but until 1300, almost no one could afford it but the very rich.

## Ruling Class

Desperate for more sugar, but with a climate that isn't ideal for the crop, Europeans took to the seas looking for new lands to plant sugar. In 1493, just a year after he first set foot in the "New World," Columbus planted sugar on the island of Hispaniola, now Haiti and the Dominican Republic.

## Stuck at Sea

## Big Islands

Greenland is the world's biggest island, and has landmass both above and below the Arctic circle.

**Green Land**

## Comfy Furniture

The first furniture in the world probably wasn't that comfortable, because it was literally made out of rocks. In ancient Egypt, padded beds were so rare that the ones used by pharaohs were easy to dismantle and transport, so they could take them with them wherever they went. It wasn't until the late 1600s that the furniture we're used to, like sofas and end tables, emerged in Europe. Before that, if people wanted to sit side by side, they had to plop down on benches, a nearby trunk, or even beds.

**Let's Go Camping**

## Stuck at Sea

When shipwrecked sailors were marooned together at sea and got hungry enough to eye each other as a possible snack, evidence suggests that, although lots were always drawn, people were most likely to be killed according to their rank—lowest first and highest last.

**Tips for Cannibals**

## Hot Water

There are about a thousand geysers around the globe today, and five hundred of them are located in Yellowstone Park. The second-biggest collection is in Russia's Valley of Geysers, but in 2007, an earthquake caused a mudslide that buried two-thirds of them.

**Yellow Stone**

## Fall Leaves

Trees in North America and East Asia turn mostly red during the fall, but trees in Europe are more likely to turn yellow, maybe because mountain ranges in North America and Asia protected insect predators from ice ages, so the trees had to keep turning red, which wards off their attacks. But in Europe, where cool temperatures killed off almost all leaf-eating insects, trees may have stopped spending the extra energy it takes to turn red. In any case, no other regions in the world get such a spectacular color show in autumn, because their climates don't have the same changes in temperature and light.

**Insect Predators**

## Insect Predators
## Honey Bees

To make a single pound of honey, bees collect the nectar of two million flowers, which means they have to fly 90,000 miles: the equivalent of circling the globe three times.

**Long Flights**

## Yellow Stone

Almost all the gold on earth got here on space rocks, crashing through our atmosphere as meteors millions of years after the planet was born.

**Long Flights**

## Green Land

Greenland's Northeast Greenland National Park is the biggest national park in the world, and the largest piece of protected land on the planet. At 375,000 square miles, it's just shy of half the size of Greenland itself, and bigger than the vast majority of other countries in the world.

**Other Planets**

## Tips for Cannibals

If you're ever marooned with a bunch of other starving people, don't bother to eat them. By the time you start thinking about snacking on your fellow humans, none of you probably have enough nutrients left in your flesh to be worth eating.

**Weird Vitamins**

## Interesting Medicine

In the Middle Ages, good European druggists would be sure to have a supply of mummy powder, composed of ground-up mummies looted from Egyptian tombs. It was thought to be both a universal cure and an aphrodisiac.

**Weird Vitamins**

Ancient Roman doctors used to prescribe the blood of vanquished gladiators to treat epilepsy.

**Weird Vitamins**

Physicians in ancient Egypt prescribed a whole catalog of animal dung to their patients, from gazelles, donkeys, and dogs. And modern science says it likely worked, because some dung does contain microflora that act as antibiotics.

**Weird Vitamins**

# Innovations of India

The English word *shampoo* comes from the Hindi *chāmpo*, because the first shampoos were invented in India, with ingredients like hibiscus and gooseberry, which both strengthened hair and prevented premature graying.

**Going Gray**

The first rulers were made in India, out of ivory, sometime before 1500 BC—and accurate down to decimals—which were also invented in India.

**Ruling Class**

# Innovations of India
# Interesting Medicine

A physician named Sushruta, from India, performed the first cataract surgeries—in the third century. His method used a curved needle to shift the clouded lens to the back of the eye, and his follow-up instructions prescribed butter to bathe the eyes until they healed. The procedure is described in his Sushruta Samhita, one of the most important books on medicine in the ancient world.

**Important Books**

## Important Books

Movable type was invented by Johannes Gutenberg in the 1440s, and by 1500, the new process was used to produce about twenty million books.

**Different Types**

## Let's Go Camping

You might think that a kid who grew up bouncing around the back of a covered wagon as his parents crossed the Great Plains would be tired of sleeping outdoors, but Thomas Hiram Holding couldn't get enough of it. As an adult, with nostalgic thoughts of his youth, he founded the world's first camping club in 1901 and wrote the first camping handbook in 1908. Americans had been sleeping in the woods for fun as early as the 1870s, but it was Holding who effectively created modern camping.

**Great Planes**

## Cute Chimps

Chimpanzees are the smartest primates on the planet, after humans. They share 98.5 percent of our DNA, and a lot of our human habits, like laughing, hugging, and caring what they look like: they spend a significant amount of their time pulling dirt and critters from each other's silky hair, which not only keeps them healthy and clean but also creates deep bonds between individuals—kind of like a trip to the salon.

**Just for Laughs**

## Great Planes
## Long Flights

In March 2020, passengers on Air Tahiti Nui, a French airline, endured the longest commercial passenger flight in history. Concerns about COVID-19 meant they couldn't make a scheduled stop in Los Angeles, so the plane flew direct from Tahiti to Paris, setting a new record at 9,765 miles in about sixteen hours.

**Cool Islands**

## Going Gray

Our hair doesn't really turn gray. If a hair grows in black, brown, or blond, that's the color it'll stay. But as our hair follicles age, they produce less color—which makes hairs look gray. Why does hair seem to gray sooner under stress? Stress can't really change the color of an individual hair. But it can make you shed your hair around three times faster than normal—which speeds up the process of it growing back in gray.

**Dumb Blondes**

## Weird Vitamins

Cornelia Kennedy, a grad student writing her thesis in 1916, was the first person to use letters to describe recently discovered "vitamines," although the professor she worked with stole the credit for years. Today, we still use vitamins A through E, then skip to vitamin K, because the original vitamins F, G, H, and I were later reclassified into other categories—and vitamin J was dropped from the list because it's only beneficial to guinea pigs.

**Famous Plagiarists**

## Different Types

Why are letters described as *uppercase* and *lowercase*? Because in the early days of printing, the different versions of the movable letters of a font were kept in different cases: some above, and some below.

**Scrabble Tiles**

## Scrabble Tiles

*Scrabble* is an acceptable word in the wildly popular board game Scrabble, which was invented by architect Alfred Butts in 1931, while he was out of work during the Great Depression. Game manufacturers weren't interested, so Butts gave entrepreneur James Brunot permission to produce it. Brunot started making twelve an hour with hand-stamped letter tiles. For several years, they ran the business at a loss, until the president of Macy's played it while he was on vacation, and placed a life-changing order. By the 1950s, demand was so high that the games had to be rationed. So what does *scrabble* mean? "To scratch or grab, trying to catch or keep hold of something."

**Bare Butts**

## Ruling Class

Qin Shi Huang, the first emperor of China, was obsessed with immortality and sent searchers far and wide at any rumor of immortal beings or potions that might extend his life. Unfortunately, many of the potions he imbibed in hopes of everlasting life were packed full of jade or mercury—which is probably what ultimately killed him.

**Immortal Beings**

## Just for Laughs

England's *Punch* magazine created the first modern cartoon, but stand-up comedy was born in America. The most stripped-down version of comedy in history, featuring only a single performer who talks directly to the audience, it was literally born among strippers: the first stand-up comics started performing between burlesque acts in New York City, in the late 1800s.

**Sucker Punch**

## Sucker Punch

Francis Ngannou, the Cameroonian French mixed martial artist, holds the record for the world's hardest punch, measured in 2017 at 96 horsepower, which feels like being hit by a sledgehammer, or a small car.

**If I Had a Hammer**

## Bare Butts

History records one of the first-ever incidents of mooning in 1203, when defeated Crusaders were sailing out of Constantinople, which they had failed to capture. On the shore, delighted Byzantine citizens didn't just yell for joy—they reportedly turned around and lifted their garments to give the departing Europeans a view of their bare butts.

**Blue Moon**

## Immortal Beings

Almost every living being ages, but some can live pretty much forever, including yeast, which will never die if the conditions are right, and jellyfish, which can regenerate indefinitely.

**French Bread**

## Other Planets

The biggest volcano in the known universe is on Mars—it's as tall as Mount Everest and as wide as Arizona, because Mars doesn't have as much gravity as Earth, so its volcanoes can grow to incredible sizes when they erupt.

**Blue Moon**

Wind speeds on Venus are hurricane-strength pretty much all the time, at about 250 miles per hour—and they only seem to be getting faster.

**Blue Moon**

Saturn isn't the only planet with rings. Jupiter, Uranus, and Neptune have them, too. But Saturn's are so spectacular they were spotted as early as the 1600s—because they're the remains of an entire moon.

**Blue Moon**

People have observed Jupiter's Great Red Spot, caused by a giant storm on the planet's surface, since the 1600s. It's only about half the size today as it was back then, but that's still pretty big: a little over 10,000 miles wide.

**Blue Moon**

Think the temperature swings are bad in Minnesota? Try Mercury, where the temperature goes up as high as 840 degrees Fahrenheit during daylight, because it's the closest planet to the sun—then drops as low as negative 275 degrees Fahrenheit at night.

**Blue Moon**

Rogue planets aren't part of any solar system—they just hurtle endlessly through space, probably after being ejected from the gravitational field of their companion star.

**Blue Moon**

## Blue Moon

One of Saturn's moons, Titan, has rain that falls on the surface, and then evaporates, just like on Earth. But that rain is not water—what falls from Titan's sky and fills its lakes would be gases on Earth but are liquids in Titan's cold temperatures: ethane and its chemical cousin methane, which is a major ingredient in farts.

**Fart Ingredients**

## Cool Islands

Gunkanjima, a Japanese island in the waters near Nagasaki, was once the most densely populated place on earth, because it sits atop an undersea coal mine and provided a home for five thousand mine workers on just sixteen acres. The mine was closed in 1974, and today, not a single resident lives there, but you can get a look at it in the James Bond flick *Skyfall*, which features the abandoned buildings as the villain's lair.

**Villainous Lairs**

## Dumb Blondes

In her movies, Marilyn Monroe may have played the most memorable ditzy blonde in history, though in real life she was anything but. She studied at the Actor's Studio, just like James Dean, Paul Newman, Robert De Niro, and Al Pacino, and her dream role was to star in a film adaptation of Dostoyevsky's *The Brothers Karamazov*, one of her favorite books.

**The Godfather**

## If I Had a Hammer

The Norse god Thor is enjoying some unexpected popularity in recent decades, largely due to a starring role in Marvel's incredibly popular movies. Guardian of Asgard, the home of the ancient gods of Norway, his name comes from the Norse word for thunder, which ancient Norwegians believed was made by the sound of his hammer. And the name of the hammer, Mjölnir, probably comes from old Slavic or Welsh words for lightning.

**Marvel Movies**

## Famous Plagiarists

The Johnny Cash biopic *Walk the Line* contains a scene of Cash writing "Folsom Prison Blues" while in the army, but in fact, Cash lifted the melody and many of the lyrics from "Crescent City Blues" by Gordon Jenkins—including the song's iconic first line: "I hear the train a-comin', it's rolling 'round the bend." Cash added his own lines about shooting a man in Reno just to watch him die, and turned the tune from a story about a woman itching to get out of a small town into one about a man who knows he might never leave prison: "And I ain't been kissed lord since I don't know when" became "And I ain't seen the sunshine since I don't know when." And he replaced the schmaltzy original arrangement with his famous driving beat. But when "Folsom Prison Blues" came out in 1969, Jenkins sued, and Cash ended up paying a hefty sum, more than half a million in today's money, to settle the case.

## Solitary Confinement

## The Godfather

Mario Puzo finished *The Godfather* in a hurry, because he wanted the final installment of his payment to go on vacation with his family to Europe. But when he got back, his editor had sold the paperback rights for $410,000, over eighty times his original advance of $5,000. It hit the bestseller lists in 1969, ultimately selling 21 million copies, then became a series of hit movies, starting with *The Godfather*, which Puzo wrote the script for without ever having penned one before. Years later, when he was asked to teach a screenwriting class, he thought he should really learn something about writing scripts and bought a book on screenwriting, only to discover that *The Godfather* was the first example the author held out for young writers to emulate.

**Long Vacations**

## Fart Ingredients

The average fart is mostly nitrogen and carbon dioxide, perhaps with some hydrogen, oxygen, and methane mixed in. But the rotten smell comes mostly from traces of sulfur, found in foods like onions, beans, and broccoli.

**Hydrogen Bomb**

## French Bread

The French Bread Law of 1993 specifies that the only ingredients allowed in French bread are flour, yeast, salt, and water, if you consider that an ingredient—and governs the weight and length of each loaf. But if you like French bread better, it might be because of something not mentioned in the law: French breads are fermented longer than American breads, which gives them a richer flavor.

**American Bread**

## Solitary Confinement

The first prison in the United States that was built primarily for putting prisoners into solitary confinement, the Eastern Pennsylvania Penitentiary, was designed and run by Quakers, who thought that the solitude would be a gift to prisoners, giving them time to reflect and repent. But modern studies show that it can lead to mental and physical deterioration, because in general, humans do better when they're together.

**Old Prisons**

## Villainous Lairs

Hitler spent almost half of World War II at Wolf's Lair, a secret command center in a Polish forest, an eighty-building compound that has lain in moss-covered ruins since the end of the war.

**Ancient Ruins**

## Long Vacations

*Vacation* in English originally referred to a summer recess for the court system. It wasn't until the Industrial Revolution that the concept of time off for the average worker emerged—because you couldn't take a vacation from planting and harvesting crops, or fighting a war.

**Telling Time**

## Ancient Ruins
## Old Prisons

Ancient Romans thought that imprisonment for life was inhumane, so instead they executed anyone convicted of a capital offense.

**Define Human**

## American Bread

In 1921, Wonder Bread rolled out its classic sliced loaves, with flour that had been specially treated to produce its signature fluffy texture—which removed most of its nutritional value. But in the 1940s, after a wave of pellagra—a disease caused by vitamin deficiency—in southern states, the government urged bread makers to add back nutrients that had been stripped away. Bread makers started touting the benefits of "enriched" bread, and pellagra cases dropped to almost zero.

**Fluffy Foods**

## Marvel Movies

Since Marvel Studios released its first film, *Iron Man*, in 2008, it has raked in an average of almost $1 billion per movie, almost three times as much as Hollywood blockbusters usually make.

**Super Human**

# Telling Time

Ancient Egyptians, perhaps the first to create the sundial, divided their days into twelve segments, much like today's twelve hours, but in ancient Rome, a week was eight days long.

**Atomic Time**

Galileo refined the modern pendulum clock after noticing how regularly a cathedral lamp swung overhead.

**Atomic Time**

In theory, a second is 1/86,400 of a solar day, or twenty-four hours, divided by sixty minutes in an hour, divided by sixty seconds in a minute. But today, seconds are defined by *atomic frequency*: how long it takes an atom of cesium to pass from one state to another—which means a second can be the same far beyond this world, even if we no longer had the cycles of the earth and sun to measure by.

**Atomic Time**

## Fluffy Foods

Cotton candy was invented in 1897 by a two-person team: candymaker John Wharton and a Nashville dentist, Dr. William Morrison, who might have been trying to drum up business. And the original name of the confection even had a dental-flavored theme: fairy floss.

**Define Human**

## Atomic Time
## Hydrogen Bomb

Atom bombs work because of the huge amount of energy released when an atom is split, but hydrogen bombs are fueled by the power released when atoms of hydrogen combine. H-bombs have been tested by both the United States and Russia since 1952, but never used in warfare, even though at the height of nuclear proliferation in the 1980s, there were an estimated forty thousand nuclear weapons, both hydrogen and atomic, in the hands of the world's nuclear powers.

**Define Human**

## Super Human
## Define Human

What makes humans different from all other animals? You might think it's the fact that we've got language, but some apes can understand and sign thousands of words, and they're not the only ones—dogs, birds, and dolphins all have the ability to understand large vocabularies as well. Is it the fact that humans have morals, a sense of fairness, and even empathy? Nope. Monkeys who see each other get different rewards for the same behavior will start to refuse the rewards—even if they're the one getting the better treat. And chimps will help each other reach food—even if they know they won't get any themselves. It's not even our technical ingenuity: humans aren't the only species to use tools. And we're not the only ones who lie: chimps do, too. But humans really are different in two big ways. First, we're much more likely than other animals to help other humans whom we don't have close connections to. And second, we're the only creatures who want to share the contents of our minds with others, through art and writing. It's helping strangers that makes us human. And what you're doing right now—reading books.

**Cool Dolphins** ▬▬▬▬▬▬▬▬▬▬▬
**Big Lies** ▬▬▬▬▬▬▬▬▬▬▬▬▬▬▬▬▬▬
**Large Vocabularies** ▬▬▬▬▬▬▬▬▬
**The Kindness of Strangers** ▬▬▬▬▬▬▬▬

## Cool Dolphins

Scientists think that dolphins might once have lived on land, because their fins seem to have functioned originally as legs with toes. If that's the case, the former land dwellers may have decided to chuck it all in for life in the ocean, which is one very interesting possible explanation for the legend of mermaids.

### Legendary Mermaids

## Large Vocabularies

Shakespeare had a huge impact on our vocabulary in English. He added over 1,700 well-used words to the language, including *swagger*, *lonely*, and *bandit*. But modern poets are still inventing new words: studies show that today's rappers invent even more original words than Shakespeare did back in his day.

**Swaggering Bandits**

## Big Lies

Has anyone ever told you that pouring oil in pasta will keep it from sticking? It's a big lie! Stirring is the secret to ward off sticky pasta. And don't bother salting the water to make it boil faster, like the old tale says. Salt adds taste, but it might actually make the water heat up *slower*.

**Yummy Pasta**

# Legendary Mermaids

Many people think mermaids were mentioned as far back as Homer's *Odyssey*, but in fact the Sirens who sang beautiful songs that lured men to their death weren't half woman, half fish, but half woman, half bird.

## Fly Like an Eagle

The Kunwinjku people of northern Australia tell stories of a mythological creature that's half female, half fish, with seaweed for hair, which can also shape-shift into a crocodile or dragonfly, and bewitch the weather.

## Bad Hair Day

Dutch sailors shipwrecked on a Korean island in the mid-1600s returned home with tales of mermaids, but there's a good chance they were based on the women who free-dived for fish and seaweed in the area. Chinese and Japanese women have been doing similar dives for at least 1,500 years and are given the name Dragon Wives for their ability to dive as deep as 90 feet, and hold their breath in freezing water for as long as three minutes—perhaps because women have more body fat than men, which helps them survive the chilly temperatures.

## Don't Hold Your Breath

## The Kindness of Strangers

In Cork County, Ireland, a sculpture composed of 20-foot-high steel eagle feathers commemorates a donation that the Native American Choctaw tribe sent to Ireland in 1847 at the height of the Irish potato famine. Members of the Choctaw Nation had suffered through a terrible tragedy of their own only a few years before, after being removed to Oklahoma from their original homeland in Mississippi. But although they were still trying to rebuild their own lives, and living in grinding poverty, the Choctaw responded to the stories of Irish suffering by sending $170 to relief efforts—about $5,000 in today's money.

**Fly Like an Eagle**

## Yummy Pasta

Italians weren't the first people to eat pasta. The Chinese were eating noodles as early as 5000 BC, while the ancestors of the first Romans didn't start until around 500 BC. But per capita, Italians do eat the most pasta in the world today.

**Big Eaters**

## Swaggering Bandits

The Dalton Gang were distant relatives of the infamous James Gang, and they weren't about to be shown up by their famous cousins. So in October 1892, they decided to rob two banks in the same town: Coffeyville, Kansas. They got away from the first bank with a pretty good haul, but as they were trying to rob the second, the good people of Coffeyville rallied and shot down every single member of the gang in the street—except the youngest Dalton brother.

**Little Brothers**

## Fly Like an Eagle

Ever wonder why it's so easy to sing along to Steve Miller Band songs? Because Steve Miller, the singer of "Fly Like an Eagle" and "The Joker," only has a vocal range of a few notes, barely an octave. And every single one of his melodies uses only those few notes.

**The Joker**

## Bad Hair Day

Punk rock kids thought they were blowing up fashion norms by dyeing their hair blue or pink in the 1980s, but just before World War I broke out, colored wigs were all the rage in Paris—in green, blue, yellow, salmon, and violet—chosen to match or contrast with the rest of an ensemble. More staid fashionistas stuck with black-and-white wigs, which came in stripes, checks, polka dots (considered a bit bourgeois), and plaid (recommended for a night at the theater).

**Loud Plaid**

## Don't Hold Your Breath

People haven't always stood in line to wait for the good stuff. In fact, the custom seems to have started during the French Revolution, when people lined up outside of bakeries to get bread. For a while, everyone thought that was just the French, acting crazy, instead of all running at the counter in a big mob like everyone else. But like many French habits, standing in line eventually caught on around the world.

**Don't Stand So Close to Me**

# Big Eaters

The Tasmanian devil can eat almost half its own body weight in just half an hour. That's the equivalent of the average American eating about fifty pizzas in the same amount of time.

## Special Delivery

Pythons' jaws aren't linked together like humans', so they can eat things that are larger than their own head—like an alligator. It just might take them months to digest it—which means they don't need to eat anything else in all that time.

## Dental Nightmares

Blue whales are the biggest animal on the planet, but they subsist on something pretty tiny: krill, a marine critter less than an inch long that kind of looks like a shrimp. But to keep up their enormous body weight, blue whales have to eat literally a ton of krill: they've been known to snarf up as many as forty million a day.

## Small Stuff

Sharks eat pretty much anything they see, even if it isn't strictly "food." They've been found with shoes, tires, license plates, burlap bags, bottles of wine, and pieces of a coat of armor stuck in their bellies.

**Coats of Armor**

Caterpillars are basically one big stomach, with skin and a circulation system wrapped around a giant gut built to consume a thousand times what they weigh in just a couple of months so that they can gather all the nutrients they need to turn into the beautiful and complex machinery of a butterfly.

**Butterfly Mechanics**

## Little Brothers

Firstborn children are more likely to turn out to be presidents or astronauts than their siblings are. But it's younger children who are most likely to want to change the world by reforming it—or come up with a scientific breakthrough that causes a revolution in the way everybody thinks, like Charles Darwin. And when those younger sibs come up with their new ideas, other younger siblings are much more likely to get on board with them than older ones are.

**That's Revolting**

## Butterfly Mechanics

All butterflies have to be mechanics, because they have to assemble their own mouths. When they emerge from the chrysalis, their long proboscises are in two pieces, so it's their job to fit the two pieces together into the single long tube that will allow them to actually slurp up the nutrients they eat.

**Dental Nightmares**

## Special Delivery

Very few people living in slavery in the United States escaped to freedom, because it was so difficult to find shelter or food in hostile country. But Henry "Box" Brown did, in 1849, by mailing himself from Virginia to abolitionists in Philadelphia with $86 he had saved working as a tobacconist. After his pregnant wife and three children were sold to a plantation owner in North Carolina, Brown had a fellow church choir member pack him into a specially made box, 3 feet by 2 feet by 2.5 feet, with three holes for breathing. Shippers treated the box so roughly that Brown was knocked out by the impact, but twenty-seven hours later, he emerged from the box in Philadelphia, where he immediately burst out singing Psalm 40: "I waited patiently for the Lord; and he heard my cry." He spent the rest of his life as a speaker, actor, singer, and magician, making hankies and pocket watches disappear into a mirrored box, until his death in 1897.

## The Sound of Music

## Loud Plaid

The family tartans of the Scottish clans date back to the Roman Empire, with the world's oldest piece of plaid found in a jar of Roman coins from the third century BC. In the beginning, Scottish clans all wore the same pattern for a simple reason: local weavers usually produced only one signature kind of cloth, so everybody had to wear it. But over time, the regional patterns took on tribal meaning, and the tribal garb spread far and wide—a red-headed mummy was recently found wearing tartan in a Chinese desert, thousands of miles from the homeland of the Celts. By the 1700s, wearing tartan was so tied with Scottish identity that wearing it in England was considered a revolutionary act for almost a century. And the proper name is *tartan*, not *plaid*. Originally, "plaid" just referred to any rectangular cloak, but because so many plaids were made from tartan, the words came to mean the same thing.

## That's Revolting

## Dental Nightmares

Humans have been getting cavities for about twenty thousand years—or pretty much ever since we started farming enough to fill up on carbs. And archaeological evidence suggests we've been drilling and filling our teeth ever since. But it wasn't until dentist Horace Wells saw a demonstration of laughing gas in 1845 that the procedures involved anesthetic. Wells watched a guy take a long breath of the gas and smash his shin on a bench—while apparently feeling no pain. The next day, Wells dosed himself with laughing gas and had a friend rip out his tooth. When Wells couldn't recall the pain, modern dental anesthesia was born.

**What Are You Laughing At?**

## Coats of Armor

Soldiers wore armor into battle for thousands of years—until the seventeenth century, when firearms got so powerful that not even a metal uniform could protect you from them.

**Funny Uniforms**

## The Joker

Playing cards began to turn up in Europe in the late 1300s, but nobody's sure where they came from, because paper is so fragile that not many ancient cards survive. But China, Egypt, Persia, India, and Korea all played cards before Europeans did.

**Just My Luck**

Cards appeared in China as early as the ninth century, when mahjong and dominoes were also making an appearance.

**Just My Luck**

Some of the first mentions of playing cards in Europe were sermons condemning them as an occasion for gambling. And according to those first mentions, the decks already appeared to have fifty-two cards.

**Just My Luck**

The first playing cards in Italy were hand-painted, and paper was so valuable at the time that nobody in Europe could afford them but the very rich.

**Just My Luck**

Italian decks featured kings, queens, and jacks, but early Spanish decks had kings, knights, and jacks—with no queens and no tens.

**Just My Luck**

The first decks in Europe had suits of swords, clubs, cups, and coins, perhaps borrowed from similar suits on Egyptian playing cards. When Germany became Europe's biggest manufacturer of playing cards, the Germans introduced their own suits: acorns, bells, leaves, and hearts. But it was the French who came up with the suits most common today: hearts, spades, diamonds, and clubs.

**Just My Luck**

## Small Stuff

What makes an electron microscope better than a regular optical microscope? How much magnification you can see has to do with the wavelength of light: the smaller the wavelength, the smaller the thing you can see. Electrons have tiny wavelengths, so they can see things a thousand times smaller than an optical microscope: like cracks in steel, which look like the Grand Canyon under an electron microscope.

**The Grand Canyon**

## Don't Stand So Close to Me

In the United States, it's polite to stand about 3 feet away from someone you don't know. In Romania and Saudi Arabia, people expect you to stay at least 4 feet away. But in Argentina, people might think you're standoffish if you do—they're used to a social distance of about 2.5 feet. Of all countries, the United States is among the most likely to make people from other cultures feel crowded—most cultures want more space from one another than Americans do.

**Slow Boat to Argentina**

## That's Revolting

To launch their revolution against the Cuban government, Fidel Castro and Che Guevara had to get to Cuba from Veracruz, Mexico, where they were living in exile. But because they were exiles, they couldn't enter through regular ports, and the only boat they could find was a yacht designed for twelve. They loaded it with over eighty people, which slowed them down so much that they arrived long after they'd planned to coordinate with other revolutionaries in Cuba. And they arrived in broad daylight, instead of under cover of darkness. Shortly after landing, Cuban government forces caught up with them, killing at least sixty in the mountains near where they'd landed. It took the handful who survived days to find each other again. But when they did, they formed the core of the forces who toppled the government two years later.

## Mountain Living

## Funny Uniforms

The official job of the guys who wear the bright red uniforms outside the Tower of London is to guard the royal jewels and keep prisoners from escaping—even though there aren't any prisoners in the tower anymore. Their official name is the Yeoman Warders, but everyone knows them as Beefeaters—maybe because French palace guards used to be called *buffetiers*, or maybe because the Yeoman Warders used to be paid, in part, in big slabs of beef.

**Tower of London**

## Just My Luck

Why do people think horseshoes are lucky? According to English legend, the devil once came to a blacksmith to get shoes for his hooved feet. But once the blacksmith nailed them on, they hurt, so the devil demanded he take them off. So the blacksmith did—but not until the devil promised never to bother a house with a horseshoe over the door.

**Speak of the Devil**

## What Are You Laughing At?

Babies laugh before they can talk—even if they're deaf or blind. And there's no culture on earth where people don't laugh. But why do we do it? For one thing, it bonds us with other humans. In a group, we're thirty times more likely to laugh than we do when we're alone—and when people listen to recordings of groups laughing, they can tell just by listening to the laughter whether the people are close friends or strangers. But it's also good for us. The bump in our blood pressure and heart rate from laughter releases tension and calms us down, and the increase in oxygen helps our heart and lungs. It boosts our immune system, by reducing stress. And it releases endorphins—which feels like happiness.

## The Sound of Music

## Slow Boat to Argentina

During the great waves of immigration from Europe to the Americas in the 1800s, most immigrants landed in the United States. But the next-hottest destination at that time was Argentina, which drew millions of mostly Spanish and Italian immigrants, as well as some who had been denied entrance to the United States.

## Strike Out

## Strike Out

Babe Ruth broke the record for hitting the most home runs in a single season in 1923—the same year he broke the record for the highest batting average in history. In fact, Ruth was the first player in baseball to consistently hit home runs, which most people saw as just a lucky fluke before he came on the scene. But to get there, he broke another record: in 1923, he also struck out more times than any other player in the league.

**The Greatest Game**

## Mountain Living

Nestled in the Andes Mountains of Peru, Lake Titicaca is the highest lake in the world that's big enough to be navigated by large boats. It's 50 miles wide, and almost 13,000 feet high. Twenty-five rivers feed into it—but only one runs out. An underwater temple, as well as ruins on its banks, indicate that it was home to one of the oldest cultures anywhere in the Americas, and Inca legend holds that it was on the lake's banks that the founders of the empire first came to earth, sent by the sun.

**Here Comes the Sun**

# Tower of London

Twenty-two people have been executed in the Tower of London, the last in 1941: a German spy who was caught after parachuting into England during World War II. But the most recognizable tower in London is the huge clock at Big Ben, just down the Thames.●●●●●●●●●●●●●

**Like Clockwork**

●●●●●●●●●●●●●●●●●●●●●●●●●●●●●●

Famous prisoners of the Tower of London include Anne Boleyn, locked up there after Henry VIII got tired of her, and Sir Walter Raleigh, who was locked up in the tower twice. The first time was for marrying one of the queen's ladies-in-waiting without permission. The second was after Queen Elizabeth's death, when her son, then king, locked him up for almost thirteen years.●●●●●

**Like Clockwork**

●●●●●●●●●●●●●●●●●●●●●●●●●●●●●●

Along with high-class prisoners, the Tower of London was home to a zoo, founded in the 1200s, featuring polar bears, elephants, and kangaroos. It only closed in 1835, when all the animals were moved to the newly opened London Zoo.

**Like Clockwork**

# The Grand Canyon

The Grand Canyon in Arizona isn't the world's only grand canyon—there's another one, Yarlung Tsangpo Grand Canyon, in Tibet, which is twice as deep and 30 miles longer. But the one in Arizona is the biggest canyon in the world, because it's so *wide*: 10 miles across at the widest parts, and big enough to swallow the entire state of Rhode Island.

**Country Roads**

The Federal Aviation Administration was created after two airplanes collided while both were trying to give passengers a good view of the Grand Canyon, in 1956.

**Danger Warnings**

The Grand Canyon is so big that it generates its own weather because of the temperature swings created by changes in elevation from the canyon floor to the rim.

**High Elevation**

The Grand Canyon is home to its own breed of snakes, not found anywhere else in the world. They're pink, to fit in with the canyon's pink-and-orange walls.

**Local Color**

## Like Clockwork

Around 300 BC, an engineer named Yan Shi astonished the Chinese royal court with an eerily lifelike mechanical man that could walk, turn its head, and sing. But when it started winking and flirting with the royal ladies, the king got furious and threatened to execute Yan Shi. To save his skin, the engineer quickly disassembled the machinery of the mechanical man, showing the king that the being that had enraged him was only made out of wood, leather, glue, and lacquer, covered with mechanical muscle, teeth, and hair. The mechanical man, Yan Shi showed the king, even came complete with internal organs, from lungs to intestines. At Yan Shi's invitation, the king removed the heart and saw that the mechanical man could no longer talk. And when the king pulled out the kidneys, the mechanical man could no longer walk. So the king's fury turned to delight, and instead of executing Yan Shi, he showered him with praise.

**Great Brains**

## Danger Warnings

The animal that's deadliest to humans on the planet—besides other humans—is the mosquito. It's responsible for giving fatal diseases, including malaria and yellow fever, to 725,000 people a year, while in all crimes and wars, humans kill about 475,000 people each year.

**Endless Buzzing**

## Speak of the Devil

The first person to go over Niagara Falls in a barrel—and live to tell about it—was sixty-three-year-old daredevil Annie Edson Taylor. Trying to make money to care for her ailing mother, Taylor made the drop because a local promoter promised to pay her, whether or not she survived. She made it over the falls without a single broken bone, but the promoter had vanished. He even stole the barrel she'd gone over the falls in, which wound up in a department store in Chicago. So Taylor found a different way to capitalize on her accomplishment: selling souvenir photos of herself.

**Old Photographs**

## The Greatest Game

The most popular sport in the world, by a huge margin, is association football—known in the United States as soccer. Four billion people, or a little over half the population of the world, consider themselves fans. And American football isn't anywhere in the top ten most popular sports worldwide. It's got less fans worldwide than cricket, field hockey, tennis, volleyball, basketball, baseball, rugby, golf—and table tennis.

**Still Kicking**

## Country Roads

The grounds around the Château de Fontainebleau, about forty miles outside Paris, became the world's first nature preserve in 1861, with the world's first hiking trails. After being dismissed from his post at the palace, Claude-François Denecourt started wandering in the woods. Without any official blessing, he created trails; dug out caves; made stairs, monuments, and underground tunnels; and built fountains. As visitors flooded the forest, he also made up legends about its landmarks and named hundreds of trees and rocks. The area became so popular, it earned its own train stop.

**Local Color**

# The Sound of Music

The human brain has a set of nerves that only react when we're listening to music.

**Great Brains**

Cyclists pedal faster when there's music playing—maybe because if they're listening to music, they don't need as much oxygen.

**Big Fans**

Dogs are calmer when they listen to classical music—but heavy metal stresses them out. Cats, predictably, don't seem to care whether humans are listening to music, or not.

**Big Fans**

Even when dementia patients forget many other things they used to know, they often know the melodies and the complete words to songs—because they're stored in a different part of the brain.

**Great Brains**

Babies react to music even in the womb, and once they're born, music helps them calm down—and eat more.

**Big Fans**

Tobacco plants and chrysanthemums both change their cell structures when they're exposed to music—and food crops like rice grow faster.

**Big Fans**

Elephants trained to play drums in Thailand turned out to be even better at keeping a steady beat than humans.

**Great Brains**

## Big Fans

Mozart sold more CDs than 2016 Grammy winners Beyoncé, Drake, and Adele—in 2016. A box set released to mark the 225th anniversary of the composer's death came out that year, containing 200 CDs—and each one of them added to Mozart's sales count.

**Unlikely Stars**

## Here Comes the Sun

In Earth's solar system, 99.8 percent of everything is . . . the sun. All the mass of all the other planets, dwarf planets, asteroids, comets, ice, and space junk in the solar system, put together, only make up that remaining two-tenths of a percent.

**Important Ingredients**

## Still Kicking

Who invented soccer? The Chinese were the first people to invent a game that involved kicking balls into nets, around 300 BC. The Aztecs and Mayans were the first on earth to play team sports, long before Columbus arrived on American shores, and they had incentive to win—in Maya culture, losers sometimes wound up as human sacrifices. But the modern sport of soccer, with its current rules, solidified in nineteenth-century England.

**Fish Nets**

## Endless Buzzing

You can't get away from mosquitoes even in the Arctic, where there are still swarms of them. They manage to survive by laying their eggs near rivers, so that when the rivers melt, all their eggs hatch at the same time.

**Arctic Turns**

## High Elevation

The thing that keeps us from building super-tall buildings isn't that we can't create the structure—it's that the taller a building gets, the more elevators you need to move people around them. And the taller you build, the more the steel rope that holds elevators together strains—which is what really creates the height restrictions on big buildings.

**Super-Tall Buildings**

## Fish Nets

Fishnet stockings emerged in the Victorian era, just after the Brothers Grimm published an obscure fairy tale about a girl who saves her father from an evil king by showing up dressed in a fisherman's net. Nobody knows for sure, but some researchers think that the fairy tale planted the idea for the style, later popularized by 1930s burlesque shows and 1950s pinups.

**Pins and Needles**

## Unlikely Stars

In 2020, Captain Tom Moore scored a number-one hit on the UK music charts the same week he turned one hundred, singing "You'll Never Walk Alone." In the process, he raised more than $55 million for Britain's National Health Service (NHS). It all started with a walk around his garden for charity, but in the midst of the COVID-19 pandemic, supporters from all over the world began to donate to his fundraiser, which led to the invitation to sing with the NHS Cares Choir—and his chart-topping hit.

**Weird Music**

## Local Color

Australia's Lake Hillier boasts a white sand beach and a bright pink surface, thanks to pink bacteria and algae in the water. But Canada's Spotted Lake (known to the indigenous people of the area as Kliluk), in British Columbia, is actually polka-dotted, with dozens of smaller pools that stick around after some of the lake water evaporates each summer.

**Big Pools**

## Old Photographs

Because not everybody could afford early cameras, traveling photographers roamed from town to town, taking pictures of celebrations or disasters for a fee. There was no "standard size" for photographs yet, so photographers cut photos to all kinds of sizes and used masks that made the image appear oval or even heart-shaped. Some photographers even tacked negatives to garden vegetables or fruit in orchards so that when the fruit was mature, it'd have an image seared into its skin by the sun.

**So Negative**

## Arctic Turns

The Arctic tern, which weighs about 4 ounces, makes the longest yearly migration of any animal in the world. They fly 44,000 miles each year, from Greenland, near the North Pole, to Antarctica at the South. Over the course of their lives, which last about thirty years, that's about 1.5 million miles. And what are they after? The same thing tourists want when they buy a ticket to Italy: at both the North and the South Poles, there's tons of the kind of food that terns love to eat.

**Tiny Birds**

## Important Ingredients

Ancient Egyptians used sodium bicarbonate to clean and preserve mummies. But thousands of years later, in the mid-1800s, a chemist in England married a woman who was allergic to yeast. He discovered that sodium bicarbonate could also be used to help baked goods rise and was safe to eat—and baking soda was born.

**Killer Allergies**

## Super-Tall Buildings

In 1987, when builders broke ground for the Ryugyong Hotel in the North Korean capital of Pyongyang, it was expected to be one of the tallest buildings in the world, with three thousand rooms and five restaurants that revolved so that guests could take in panoramic views, and scheduled to open in two short years. But it took five years just to reach its full height and another sixteen years to put any windows in. Today, LED lights turn it into a nighttime attraction—but it's still unfinished: it hasn't ever hosted a single guest, and it's the tallest unoccupied building in the world.

**Stained Glass**

## Pins and Needles

One of the more perplexing passages in the Christian gospels is Jesus's colorful statement in Matthew 19:24: "It is easier for a camel to go through the eye of a needle than for a rich man to enter the kingdom of heaven." Turns out, the striking image might be due to a textual error: change just one letter, and instead of the Greek word *kamelon*, for "camel," you have the Aramaic word *kamilon*, "rope." So Jesus may have been talking about trying to put a rope through the eye of a needle, not a camel. In either case, not easy.

**Pink Elephants**

## Big Pools

Russia's Lake Baikal holds more water than all five of Michigan's Great Lakes put together. It's deeper than any other lake in the world, and also older—scientists say it was formed over 25 million years ago.

**Under Water**

## Weird Music

When parts of the Croatian seaside town of Zadar were destroyed during World War II, its citizens decided to repair the city's coastline with a set of marble stairs placed atop a series of musically tuned tubes that work as a sea organ and play harmonic sounds each time the waves hit.

**Miracle Sewers**

## Tiny Birds

The ruby-throated hummingbird weighs less than a U.S. quarter, but it's not the world's tiniest bird. That honor goes to Cuba's bee hummingbird, believed to be the smallest warm-blooded creature in the world. They got their name because they're so small, people often think they're bees.

**To Be or Not to Be**

## So Negative

People with type O-negative blood are known as universal donors, because anyone else can accept their blood—including, apparently, mosquitoes, which are twice as likely to bite people with type O blood than type A.

**Big Givers**

## Great Brains

Your whole brain works on less than 25 watts of electricity, barely enough to power a light bulb—if it's low wattage, and LED. But even the slowest thought moves through our minds at over 150 miles per hour.

### Get Smart

Stress makes you stupid, and so does alcohol. Both of them damage your ability to form memories.

### Pink Elephants

Exercise makes you smarter, by releasing chemicals that make it easier to learn.

### Good Sports

Scientists estimate that your brain has 2.5 million gigabytes of storage—vastly more than any commercial computer on the market.

### Get Smart

## Great Brains

Our brains comprise about 3 percent of our total body weight—but they get about 30 percent of our blood.

**Get Smart**

Our brains are 60 percent fat—one of the fattiest organs in our bodies.

**Fatty Food**

Our brain waves are bigger when we're asleep than awake. Alpha and beta waves, which dominate our waking life, have shorter amplitude than theta waves, which kick in when we fall asleep and start to dream.

**Pink Elephants**

Everything we do changes our brain—and we're still making new neurons, until the day we die.

**Get Smart**

## Pink Elephants

Cows, horses, and elephants are the sloppy drunks of the animal kingdom. They don't get much fruit or nectar in their diets, so the sugar in alcohol goes straight to their heads. Animals who do eat a lot of nectar and fruit—like fruit bats, bonobos, and gorillas—are the best at holding their liquor.

**Pink Birds**

## Miracle Sewers

The population of ancient Rome at its height was probably around one million people, and it took almost 1,700 years for any other city to boast numbers that big. The first one to do it: London, which doubled in size between 1700 and 1800, and cracked one million people in the early years of the nineteenth century, then continued to around eight million today. The cornerstone of all that growth? The world's first urban sewage system, over 1,000 miles of tunnels designed by Sir Joseph Bazalgette, which solved the most pressing problem of urban growth: what to do with all that human waste.

**Big Cities**

## Pink Birds

Flamingos usually flock in groups of a dozen or so, but when resources are plentiful, their flocks get bigger—as many as a million have gathered on the banks of Lake Bogoria, in Africa's Rift Valley.

**Out of Africa**

## Good Sports

If apple blossoms get fertilized by pollen from another tree, the tree you planted will produce a very different fruit—a process called "sporting." If you want an identical apple, you need to take a cutting from the original tree. Same's true for tulips, which are just as unpredictable when grown from seeds.

**Plants You Can't Trust**

## Under Water

The world's oldest shipwreck has been lying at the bottom of the Black Sea for almost 2,500 years. The 75-foot Greek merchant ship has never been disturbed because it lies more than a mile underwater, so its steering mechanism and rowing benches are still recognizable. But no one's sure what it was carrying, or to where.

**Sea Monsters**

## Out of Africa

More languages are spoken in Africa than on any other continent—around three thousand. And the country with the most official languages in the world is also on the continent: South Africa, with eleven.

**Language School**

## Killer Allergies

About 2 percent of people are allergic to exercise: even mild exertion can result in hives, an upset stomach, a runny nose, or—on the extreme end of the spectrum—a closing throat and life-threatening drops in blood pressure. And when you donate your organs, you might be donating your allergies. It's rare, but some recipients of organs have developed the same allergies as the donor.

**Big Givers**

## Fatty Food

Humans are the only primate that have a steady diet of animals bigger than us. That's how we got such big brains, relative to other animals: from the huge load of nutrients in our ancient high-fat diet.

**Small Fry**

## Get Smart
## Language School

The oldest university in the world is in Africa: the University of al-Qarawiyyin, founded in Fez, Morocco, in AD 859. Europe's first university wasn't founded until more than two hundred years later: the University of Bologna, which opened its doors in 1088.

**International Intelligence**

## Stained Glass

Mexico City has historically been one of the richest cities in the world, so the standard luxuries of a theater, like velvet curtains and a red carpet, weren't enough for its Palace of Fine Arts: it boasts a Tiffany stained-glass curtain that fills the whole stage, from the wooden boards to the top of the proscenium arch. Made from two hundred panels of glass and weighing 27 tons, the curtain depicts the two volcanoes that overlook Mexico City. Before each show, the entire scene retracts into the ceiling above the stage. But after the final bow, the glass landscape is put back in place and a light show gives the illusion of the sun rising and setting over the glass mountains.

**The Red Carpet**

## Sea Monsters

The real star of *Jurassic Park III* is the *Spinosaurus*, whose fossil was first discovered in the 1930s in Egypt—and then promptly blown up in the course of World War II. It took almost a hundred years to unearth another full skeleton, this time in Morocco. But that discovery added a twist to the tale, so to speak: the new specimen clearly had a paddle-shaped tail, which scientists say prove that it knew how to swim.

**In My Bones**

## Big Cities

Tokyo is the world's largest city, with more than 37 million people. That's more than the entire population of Canada—crammed into one thousandth of the space. It has the largest economy of any city in the world, too—bigger than New York City's, and bigger than the major Chinese urban centers of Shanghai, Beijing, and Guangzhou combined.

**Center of the Earth**

## Plants You Can't Trust

The seemingly innocuous rhododendron bush, with its broad shiny leaves and bright spring flowers, is actually full of poison, and even the Roman army wasn't immune. In the first century BC, Roman soldiers got nauseous and confused after snacking on Turkish honey—which historians now believe was probably made from rhododendron nectar. It's one of the first stories of mass poisoning in history, and it wasn't the only time that humans suffered from eating "mad honey" made from the poisonous plant. But today, the most dangerous plant in the world is probably tobacco, which kills about five million people a year.

**Sweet Thing**

## Small Fry

A tuna mother can lay over a million eggs, but the odds aren't good for any of them. Not all eggs will hatch, and most of the fry that do won't make it to adulthood. Only one in a hundred eggs will successfully navigate the tricky journey to becoming an adult fish.

**Good Odds**

# Red Carpet

The famous red carpet that celebrities walk to get to movie premieres or the Oscars isn't just a Hollywood invention. It dates back all the way to ancient Greece, when Agamemnon's wife, Clytemnestra, covered his path with red carpets to welcome him home from the Trojan War. Agamemnon worried that the lavish display would draw the ire of the gods, and maybe it did: Clytemnestra and her lover murdered him at his welcome-home dinner. Scarlet was an expensive dye, so red became known as the color of kings, and a status symbol in early America, where riverboats welcomed presidents and luxury train cars welcomed elite guests by rolling out the red carpet. Hollywood mavens were just following the ancient tradition when they rolled out their first red carpet in the 1920s, for a premiere of *Robin Hood* with Douglas Fairbanks at the Egyptian Theatre—then started using red carpet at the Oscars in 1961.

**Cabinet of Wonders**

## International Intelligence

In its early days, the fledgling literary magazine known as *The Paris Review* got a secret infusion of cash from an unlikely source: the CIA, which thought that showing off American literary accomplishments would build affection for U.S. citizens globally. Its writers would probably have been furious to know who was funding them—but there's a real chance the now-venerable institution wouldn't have survived without the help of the CIA.

**To Be or Not to Be**

## Sweet Thing

The sweetest thing in the world isn't actually a sugar but a protein. Originally discovered in West Africa's katemfe fruits, thaumatin is two thousand times sweeter than sucrose—what we call sugar. It grows in fleshy red fruits on plants over 10 feet tall with leaves a foot and a half wide. And it's got its own distinctive flavor: a slow build of sweetness, with a finishing taste like licorice.

**Magic Anise**

## In My Bones

Babies are born with 300 distinct bones, which fuse together as children grow, so that by the time we reach adulthood, the average human only has 206—most of which are in our feet and hands.

**Cabinet of Wonders**

Having a skeleton isn't all that common in the animal world—90 percent of animals don't.

**Good Odds**

Teeth are stronger than bones: they're built to sustain more damage and exert more force. But pound for pound, both teeth and bones are stronger than steel.

**Cabinet of Wonders**

In adults, about 10 percent of our bone is replaced each year—which means we have a whole new skeleton every ten years.

**Cabinet of Wonders**

## Center of the Earth

The Earth's core is thousands of miles underground, so nobody's really sure what's down there. But based on seismic data, scientists believe it's made of pure iron, about 1,500 miles wide and over 5,000 degrees Fahrenheit. In other words, it's the size of the moon, but about as hot as the surface of the sun. And scientists think it's solid, not liquid, because of the enormous pressure it's under.

**Cabinet of Wonders**

## Magic Anise

Anise, the main flavor in licorice, tastes so much like fennel that you might think they grow from the same root. They don't, but they're from the same family of plants. Fennel you can eat whole—bulb, stems, and fronds—while in general, people only eat the seeds of the true anise plant. And humans aren't the only creatures who enjoy its flavor: anise seeds are like catnip, for dogs.

**Cabinet of Wonders**

## Big Givers

The Taj Mahal might be the world's best-known monument to love: Shah Jahan, emperor of the Mughal dynasty of Northern India, built it to honor his third wife, Mumtaz Mahal. The complex of beautiful white marble buildings, surrounding an iconic pool, took an estimated twenty thousand workers twenty-two years to complete. That's because the site was finished with incredible detail, like mosaics made not from shards of glass or pottery but semiprecious stones. The name Taj may come from the Persian for "crown," since the architect, Ustad Ahmad Lahauri, was Persian, not Indian. But hauntingly, Mumtaz Mahal never got to see her husband's incredibly grand gesture of love: She never even knew about it. The year before construction began, she died while delivering the couple's fourteenth child. Deep in grief, Shah Jahan ordered construction begun on the site to serve as her tomb—and, eventually, his own.

**True Love**

## True Love

You might have heard that swans mate for life. But they're not the only loyal romantics in the animal kingdom. A dizzying array of other animals do as well, including seahorses, gray wolves, barn owls, bald eagles, black vultures, and beavers.

**A Dizzying Array**

## Good Odds
## To Be or Not to Be

Ever wonder what the odds are that life would exist on the planet Earth? Recent studies suggest that, of the 700 quintillion planets in the known universe, there may only be one like ours. An equation that calculates all kinds of factors—including the possibility of extraterrestrial life, the possibility that extraterrestrial life might be intelligent, how fast stars form in a galaxy, and the odds that the elements for life will actually come to life—estimates the odds might be more like one in a trillion trillion. But so far it's been impossible to accurately calculate, since we're missing so many of the key numbers due to another crucial factor: our ignorance.

**A Dizzying Array**

## Cabinet of Wonders
## A Dizzying Array

Before public museums became common, nobles and academics created wonder cabinets: collections of art, antiques, specimens of animals and plants, souvenirs from travel, and books, both old and new. The first illustration of a wonder cabinet on record was printed in a 1599 book called *Dell'Historia Naturale* (*Of Natural History*) by Ferrante Imperato. The engraving featured a room full of books with a ceiling covered with preserved fish arranged around a giant, dangling stuffed crocodile, surrounded by shelves dotted with shells, birds, coral, and stones. As European empires expanded, middle-class citizens began to keep wonder cabinets of their own, filled with curiosities from distant lands. These collections eventually stoked the museum craze of the Victorian age, when Elias Ashmole, who wanted his wonder room to be available to the public, donated it to Oxford University in 1683. His gift spurred big private collections, like the British Museum, the Louvre, and the Prado, to open to the public for the first time—which led to the creation of even more public museums. But whether wonder cabinets filled entire rooms or were only small treasure chests in private homes, every collection was a celebration of all the wonders of the world.

## Old Books

For the intrepid Dave Hicks

An imprint of Macmillan Publishing Group, LLC
120 Broadway, New York, NY 10271
OddDot.com

Editors: Daniel Nayeri & Sam O'Brien
Designer: Tae Won Yu

ISBN 978-1-250-25497-9
LCCN 2022017591

Our books may be purchased in bulk for promotional, educational,
or business use. Please contact your local bookseller or the Macmillan
Corporate and Premium Sales Department at (800) 221-7945 ext. 5442
or by email at MacmillanSpecialMarkets@macmillan.com.

First edition, 2023

Printed in Singapore

1 3 5 7 9 10 8 6 4 2

Joyful books for curious minds